An Unschooling Experience

MARTA OBIOLS
LLISTAR

Published by Argyle Fox Publishing
argylefoxpublishing.com

Publisher holds no responsibility for content of this work. Content is the sole responsibility of the author.

ISBN 978-1-953259-11-0 (Paperback)
ISBN 978-1-953259-12-7 (Hardcover)
ISBN 978-1-953259-13-4 (Ebook)

ARGYLE FOX
PUBLISHING

CONTENTS

To my three children,
who made me a better educator.

INTRODUCTION

I planned, and God laughed.

This is truly the story of my life. More often than not, when I plan—or rather, dream and wish, life brings me other plans I didn't wish for or dream of. As a result, I've become quite good at making lemonade with all the lemons life has thrown at me. However, I now see my life incidents were not lemons at all. They simply felt that way at the time.

I didn't wish to carry children in my womb, yet I carried two.

I never dreamed of being a stay-at-home mom, yet I now cherish the opportunity.

I never wished for my kids to be raised without school, yet it happened.

I've never considered writing a book, yet here I am, spilling my stories to you.

What did I dream and wish for? What were my heart's desires? I wanted a princess wedding and the opportunity to work as a teacher helping kids in the pediatric ward at a hospital. Neither dream came true.

But I would be a liar if I pretended none of my dreams were realized. I always wanted to grow my family through adoption and not conception. And I strongly wanted to come to America to be immersed in the English language. I am so grateful these two events happened.

Why I Wrote 18

This book focuses on unschooling. But its purpose is not to teach you how to unschool. Rather, it is to show you what unschooling looks like in one particular family. If you want to learn how to unschool, I strongly suggest John Holt's books or other books more specific on how to unschool. We're all different, and the more you read about unschooling, the better understanding you'll have. My book is my personal story as an unschooling mom.

Never in a million years did I plan or dream to stay home with my kids and homeschool them instead of entering the workforce. I feel exactly like Glennon Doyle explains in her book *Untamed*, in which she reveals that she is like the cheetah who was tamed to act like a Labrador and finally untamed herself.

I was tamed to go to college and get a job. I did both and became a very successful working mom. I sent my kids to school. Yet, when I realized that I was able to stay home with my kids, that this "old-fashioned act" was a choice, I untamed myself. As an untamed cheetah, I don't act like a dog anymore, pursuing a career. Instead, I focus on unschooling my kids, which is my true nature.

Now that my oldest kid is eighteen years old and unschooling was a success, I would like to share my story with you.

Every mom I know gets sentimental or teary-eyed when their children turn another year older. Some women even ask, "Why can't they stay little forever?"

I loved every moment as my eldest got older. I was happy every year he grew and matured. When he turned eighteen I felt like I arrived at the final line of a long marathon. I made it, he made it, we made it safely.

My son just turned eighteen, and this is our story.

HOW IT ALL STARTED

Mama," Afrika said, "I'm not learning anything."
The short sentence shocked me. My
daughter, a seven-year-old first grader, wanted
to learn. Wasn't she happy just being a kid? Why did she
want to learn? I don't remember wanting to learn anything at that age.

Good for you! my little seven-year-old self thought.

But then the grown-up in me kicked in. My mom instinct to protect took over. How heartbreaking that this
little seven-year-old booger wanted to learn and wasn't
given the opportunity. She craved knowledge and wasn't
getting any at her public school.

Afrika explained that she spent a lot of time with
her arms crossed on the table, head down. Because every
time a kid behaved badly, the whole class was punished.
For punishment, everyone had to put their heads down.

AN UNSCHOOLING EXPERIENCE

Hearing this was the last drop. It was time to leave public school and jump on the homeschool bandwagon.

***

Let me start from the beginning. When I was twenty-three years old, I became an undocumented immigrant. Initially, I came legally to America from Barcelona. For a year, I worked in a daycare with the proper paperwork. Unfortunately, my time to stay legally in the US expired.

When it was time for me to leave the country, I met Brian, my future husband. Our meeting led to my decision to extend my welcome in the US illegally. I wasn't going to allow bureaucracy, laws, rules, and governments to decide my future. But that's for another book and another day.

Since I was undocumented, I wasn't allowed to legally work. This forced my teaching career to go on pause. I then became a nanny to a wonderful family with a Canadian father and American-Turkish mother .

While I was a nannying newlywed, I unexpectedly became pregnant. Fortunately, I had a great relationship with the family for whom I nannied. They allowed me to continue working for them with my baby boy tagging along.

Day after day, I took care of their three kids and my infant, Jaume. How fortunate to spend my baby's first year with him, twenty-four seven! I was able to breast-feed him as long as my breasts allowed. I was able to witness every single milestone. And I saved money by not placing him in daycare while at work.

When the family didn't need me anymore and I was finally able to work legally, I found another job. I was hired at a daycare, where I enrolled Jaume in the toddler room.

Working in that daycare was the first red flag of many. A wake-up call. I was very disappointed to see early childhood teachers handling the preschoolers so ignorantly wrong. They sprayed children with a water bottle to correct behavior. Threatened kids with a belt. Put disobedient toddlers in a closet for time out.

I was indignant.

My degree in special education allows me to work in a variety of school settings. In my home country of Spain, teachers must have a teaching degree in early childhood education from a university to work in the early childhood education field. The daycare teachers I knew back home, including my cousin Ariadna, are loving, caring, and patient. They understand that young children misbehave and make mistakes. They know about the damage physical or psychological abuse has on a child.

However, I quickly learned that daycares in Atlanta, Georgia, are full of teachers without a degree. Few have any knowledge of early childhood education. Those who do gain their knowledge from the director of the daycare, who helps teachers educate themselves to earn a degree or get a certification. But let me assure you, I saw plenty of teachers not apply the lessons taught in the continuing education classes and teacher workshops.

AN UNSCHOOLING EXPERIENCE

Another red flag waved at me when Jaume entered kindergarten. A new charter school opened in our neighborhood, an International Baccalaureate. As a foreigner, I was very interested in my kid attending an international school instead of the regular American public school. Even though the school didn't teach Spanish, they taught Mandarin, and I liked their philosophy. I appreciated everything they stood for.

So I decided to enroll my son. Actually, I was so excited about the school, I applied to work there and was hired as a kindergarten teacher.

Just like the daycare and other Atlanta schools I'd worked for, I noticed something. Schools tend to look great on paper. They have a great philosophy, they use a wonderful curriculum, it seems so cool, so great, so innovative, blah blah blah . . . But in reality, the promises made are all lies.

My mom, a woman with a very successful career, once told me that I see all the negatives in the school because I work on the inside. "If you were just a parent on the outside," she insisted, "you wouldn't see all the troubles."

Dear Mom, I refuse to be a blinded parent.

Kindergarten year was very frustrating. I did my best as a kindergarten teacher, giving my all, putting my job first and my family second. While I did my best, my son's kindergarten teacher did not. She missed a lot of days during the school year, and parents started to protest. This teacher was so bad that her lack of work ethic eventually got her fired.

A substitute teacher was hired while the school looked for the right candidate for this class full of kindergartners. The hunt took some time, but finally, the right, sweet teacher came along.

What a disaster for my son's first school year! He missed the precious kindergarten year of bonding with a sweet, lovely teacher. Instead, he had three. I was so sad that when he finally had a taste of a good and professional educator (his new kindergarten teacher), the school year ended. Kindergarten was over, and it was time for first grade.

Unfortunately, first grade brought bad luck once again. Jaume's teacher missed a lot of days, leaving the class with a substitute teacher, day after day. It was a long, depressing year, and we were ready for a change.

After witnessing those two pathetic school years, I decided to move him to another school for second grade. The new charter school was going through growing pains from being only three years old, and I didn't want to be part of it any longer. My son's two first years of school had been such a disaster. So we ditched the charter school and decided to give the regular American public school a chance.

Second grade was fantastic. Hallelujah! Jaume had the best teacher in our short history of teachers. On top of that, the school had an amazing library, computer lab, and science lab. Jaume was involved in a variety of activities. He was in the chess club and robotics club. He even participated in the spelling bee and almost won!

Mr. Shipman was the perfect teacher for my son. I

have a precious memory when he made me cry tears of mama love. I was dropping Jaume off for class, when Mr. Shipman called to me.

"Come here," he said. "I want you to know I see your son."

What? What was he talking about?

I didn't understand at first. Then Mr. Shipman looked straight into my eyes with certainty, tenderness, and care. "I see him," he said.

Oh, dear—I cried so much! All at once, I unloaded the pain—all the pain—from the previous years. In the past my son hadn't been seen by teachers. My Jaume was the invisible kid. To hear that he was seen was overwhelming.

Once, when Jaume was in private pre-K, the school had a fire drill. Everyone exited the building. Everyone except my son. He was left behind, playing with PLAYMOBILs in the classroom all by himself. He didn't follow the kids or the teacher out of the classroom, and the teacher didn't realize he was missing. That's how invisible my boy was. But this exceptional second grade teacher *saw* him. What a great year we had with Mr. Shipman!

Regrettably, that same year, I made the mistake of taking my daughter, Afrika, out of the perfect daycare program. There, both her teachers were fantastic. But I was looking for ways to save some money, so I enrolled her in Georgia's free pre-K program.

At the time, the move was justified. After all, daycare is outrageously expensive. We were in the middle of adopting a child from Ethiopia, and the bills were growing bigger and bigger. We needed a break. Sadly, this financial break jeopardized Afrika's happiness. Those teachers at the free pre-K did unspeakable things. Fortunately, they were eventually fired and the pre-K was shut down. At least other parents and children wouldn't suffer at their hands.

In September 2010, my husband, Brian, and I traveled to Addis Ababa, Ethiopia, to get our three-year-old son, Konji. Before our trip, Brian and I agreed that I would not work after bringing Konji home. Instead, I would stay home with Konji so we could bond. The Children's Place in Ethiopia had been enough daycare experience for Konji. Our youngest child would not attend daycare in America. This was the time for bonding with his new family.

Since I was staying home and Afrika was miserable at her pre-K, we kept her home as well. I was blind to the signs life was giving me. I was a mother at home with a three-year-old and a five-year-old, and I loved it. I adored it.

While Jaume was on a roll of good teachers and good years (third grade was another nice experience), it was time for my second child to enter kindergarten.

Afrika had a different experience with daycare. She was only two months old when I parted with her. Thankfully she attended the daycare where I worked at the time. The infant room had lovely teachers. But when I left this particular daycare to work at a school to teach kindergarten, I had to find a new place closer to home and work in order to make life easier for Brian and me.

AN UNSCHOOLING EXPERIENCE

I was fortunate to be offered a deal by one of the parents in my kindergarten class. This mom had a small daycare business in her home. She offered to keep Afrika during the day and to bring her to me when she came to pick up her children from school. As a result, Afrika had a great preschool experience in this small family-owned preschool. She formed a wonderful bond with both of the teachers.

Gratefully, my girl also had the best kindergarten year. The best! Mr. Weems was so knowledgeable and resourceful, and we couldn't have asked for a better teacher.

However, things soon took a turn for the worse. The next year brought change in the Atlanta Public School System. Not only did we deal with the Atlanta cheating scandal in 2009, but also some schools were closing. Students were being sent to new schools. Our outstanding principal, who was the life and spirit of the school, left for another job opportunity. The amazing, talented school librarian adored by everyone also left also for another job opportunity. Other excellent teachers did the same. Because when you're an amazing teacher, a fantastic librarian, or a phenomenal principal, better job offers come to you. When they do, you can't refuse them. Unfortunately, the ones left behind struggle with the consequences.

The next school year, fourth and first grades, were different. The school was different. Jaume's fourth-grade teacher was one of those teachers with a great reputation. She was beloved by everyone. But she was at the end of her pregnancy. At the beginning of the school year, she went on maternity leave. Once again, my son had a substitute teacher. Things weren't better for Afrika. Now in first grade, she was unsatisfied and regularly complained she wasn't learning anything.

That year, 2012, I made the decision to remove my kids from school. I was tired of leaving their education in someone else's hands.

Their school years from kindergarten to fourth grade taught me a lesson. You can get the best teacher one year, only to get the worst teacher the next year. All this while others get stuck with a regular, mediocre teacher. I also learned that the government changes things around whenever they choose. I saw this firsthand.

Jaume had the opportunity to receive enrichment classes like music, art, and Spanish more than once a week during his school years. But Afrika suffered from the government's education cuts. As a result, she didn't receive music, art, or Spanish classes. Sadly, public school is a gamble, and I was tired of the government gambling with my kids' education. I wanted the best education for my kids, and I couldn't afford to pay tuition for my three kids to attend private school.

Initially, I was pessimistic. I wanted my kids in school. I didn't want to homeschool. To persuade myself to homeschool, I reminded myself that I was doing most of the education work anyway.

Every day, I was helping the kids with homework, Googling things I didn't understand, and finding book after book in my Kindle every night for my seven-year-old to read—or rather, devour. I've never seen a seven-year-old read a whole chapter book in a single night, night after night. Afrika did. She read all twenty-seven Junie B. Jones books in no time.

I knew I could homeschool the first grader and the preschooler easily, but I was terrified of homeschooling a fourth grader, a grade with which I had no experience. To convince myself that I was capable of homeschooling my older son, I asked myself a question.

What would you do if you were hired tomorrow to teach fourth grade?

Then I got online. I started researching what fourth graders do and learn. And I purchased a few fourth-grade books from Barnes & Noble.

During the winter break crisis of homeschool or not homeschool, a friend said, "What's important is, can you handle your kids twenty-four seven?"

That was the perfect question. It made me realize that I could homeschool. Because I love being with my kids during summer break, spring break, fall break, and winter break. I do. I really do.

I remember meeting with my sister-in-law Stacey. A native New Yorker with a successful career, Stacey sat across from me while the kids played in the Chick-fil-A play area.

"What's going on?" she asked. "What's that about you going to homeschool?"

I started to cry. Bawling. All my fears and doubts and anger came out of my body in tear form. I told her I was scared. Very scared. I explained that I didn't want to homeschool, but I had to.

She said, "Marta, you're the kind of mom that takes the kids to Mexico all summer school break to work in a rural school. You'll do great."

I'll always cherish those encouraging words.

And she was right. Why was I afraid? Every summer I came up with great educational activities and opportunities for my kids. Once I even created a summer camp at my own home. My kids loved it! All I had to do was get to know the uncharted territory called homeschooling.

THE FIRST YEARS

On December 14, 2012, Connecticut suffered a tragedy. Children, ages six and seven—kindergartners and first graders at Sandy Hook Elementary, were shot to death by a stranger. Following the horrific event, Americans were shocked. Suddenly, articles began showing up on the internet about what to do if you wanted to take your kids out of school and homeschool them. Those articles gave me guidance and clarity. They led me to decide that my children would not return to school after the Christmas break.

It's scary when you don't go with the flow of society and go against the majority of the population. When you're the minority and it's your first time becoming an outsider, you need some guidance.

Thank goodness for all the homeschool articles on the internet. These articles gave me step-by-step guidance. Through them, I learned how to disenroll students from a school, how to choose an educational method or curriculum to follow, and the importance of finding a homeschool group.

Here in Georgia, all I had to do was go to the Georgia Department of Education's website. In just a few clicks, my kids were officially and legally out of the school system. The main document needed to make it happen is a Declaration of Intent.

If interested in following me, find your state's Declaration of Intent online and print it out at home. Then fill in your kids' names and ages, your home address, and the school year when you plan to remove them from the system. Easy, peasy! With this document, which you must fill out every year, you prove that you are legally homeschooling your kids. Don't want to go back to the school to say goodbye? You don't have to.

When I told my kids they didn't have to go back to school, they couldn't believe it. Not going to school was unheard of. They had no idea not going to school was an option. My poor older son even told me, "If I knew not going to school was a choice, I would have asked you a long time ago to take me out."

Poor thing. I didn't know either.

During our first homeschooling years, I set up my dining table as a classroom. When the kids were in bed at night, I put school work on the table. The next morning when they went to eat breakfast, they would find the work easily instead of getting distracted.

In those years, the kids ate breakfast and right away

got to work. They did all kinds of school work that I found on the internet or in the books I bought in a hurry at Barnes & Noble. We followed those books like a teacher does in school. The only difference was we weren't at school. We were at home.

As a result of homeschooling, the dining room looked like an elementary school classroom. Literacy and math work hung on the walls. A history timeline stretched around the entire room. Plants were being grown and studied. A thermometer outside the window was used to observe and record data.

Looking back, I'm ashamed. Those first days were literally like a school in my home. I didn't know any better.

Don't get me wrong. There's no harm in having a rich educational environment in your living room. On the contrary, it's very beneficial. It's just that every moment in life is a teachable moment. There's no need to have it all crammed in one room. Most importantly, play-time is children at work.

I read somewhere that parents who are not teachers are really good at unschooling. Though it took me a while to deschool myself, I eventually got rid of those teacher thoughts. Slowly and steadily, I became less of a teacher and my home became less of a school. I read a few books about homeschooling and unschooling, and I learned much by reading John Holt's books.

Since I quit working and I wasn't bringing home any income, we were quite broke. So I had to be creative with our activities. At the time, my kids were ages five, seven, and nine—all really good and enjoyable stages of child development. To make our money stretch, we found activities all over Atlanta for free.

The library offers activities for free. Not only do they have plenty of books, audiobooks, ebooks, magazines, and free classes online, but they also offer activities on important holidays like Valentine's Day, Halloween, and Easter. Our library also provides activities surrounding important events like Black History Month.

The Children's Museum was free one Tuesday a month, and we took advantage. This offered space for my kids to do art with paint, play with moon sand, and build with gigantic blocks. They were able to dress up, play with a train set, pretend to shop in a child-sized supermarket, perform science experiments, learn about their bodies, and enjoy live shows.

Thanks to free passes given to us by the library, the zoo was also free. While the rest of the world is at work and school, the zoo is practically empty. Without the crowds, we could spend quality time reading the educational signs in front of each habitat. This was a great learning experience.

Additionally, we would go to Barnes & Noble, where the kids would spend hours on that carpeted floor reading books. At Barnes & Noble, it was easier to peruse books than the public library. While there, I often used my phone and Barnes & Noble's free Wi-Fi to check the library catalog. If the library had the book my kid wanted, I wouldn't buy it. I would borrow it from the library. (Sorry, Barnes & Noble. I was very broke!)

Many of our friends had memberships to The Fernbank Museum and The Atlanta History Center. When they were visiting the museum or history center, these friends would let us tag along for free. Many smart, frugal parents ask for museum, zoo, and aquarium memberships for birthday or Christmas gifts. Another great way to pay for such memberships is with tax return money.

The Fernbank Science Center was free too. They have an amazing library, and their planetarium was very affordable. The High Museum of Art admission was free one Saturday a month, offering exposure to artists from around the world, including Frida Kahlo, Picasso, Monet, and Andy Warhol.

As an added perk, a lot of the places I mentioned offer a homeschool day. On these days, homeschoolers from all over Atlanta and the surrounding areas meet for some kind of workshop or structured educational event.

We visited so many places in Atlanta. At the Museum of Design Atlanta, we watched a 3-D printer for the first time, mesmerized as it created a bracelet. Inside the Federal Reserve Bank Monetary Museum, we saw money being printed. I nearly fainted at the Carlos Museum at Emory University when I realized I was so close to real mummies. For those unable to physically get to these locations, a lot of them offer educational websites and virtual tours. These thoughtful touches make homeschool life so much easier.

A very smart mom who was at the finish line of unschooling her three teenagers once told me to expose the kids to everything possible. Go to restaurants all over town and take in any activity the city offers. Travel to every state, try all kinds of sports, go to summer camps, and sign up for after-school activities until your kids find their passion. I took her advice.

Those first years I exposed my kids and myself to everything Atlanta had to offer for free. It was a good start.

Free classes at the County Performing Art Centers gave the kids an outlet for creative writing, photography, dancing, theater, ceramics, and more. Lowe's offered a free woodwork activity on the weekends, which Jaume really enjoyed. During the spring, Emory University and the Atlanta Track Club offered a running track program that Afrika and Konji absolutely loved!

The parks, rivers, lakes, and lakes-turned-beaches were all free. We rode bikes at Grant Park. When that park became too little for us, we moved on to Piedmont Park. Eventually, we took on all the bike paths and mountain bike paths around Atlanta.

We spent monumental hours at Constitution Lakes, where I sat and enjoyed a book or a chat with a friend, as the kids wandered off in their rubber boots to investigate the world around them. They always came back nasty, muddy, and so happy and full of joy.

Thank goodness the public swimming pool also has free hours, because I can't live without a pool. Panola Mountain has so much to offer as well. That's where Afrika fell in love with tree climbing and Jaume discovered his love for archery.

Lastly, my absolute favorite free activity: Six Flags. That's right. We went to Six Flags Over Georgia without purchasing a single ticket! How? Through their amazing program, Read to Succeed. With Read to Succeed, students and teachers earn free tickets just for reading. And if you haven't heard, Pizza Hut has a similar program. Called BOOK IT!, the program allows students to earn a free pan pizza by reading books.

We did every free activity we could find in Atlanta. We even found a store named Atlanta Free Store. There, volunteers did a tremendous work. Any food heading to the dumpster at local grocery stores was salvaged. It was then gathered at Atlanta Free Store and given to people like me. Thanks to Atlanta Free Store, we often ate for free. I even got cute new clothes at no cost!

Because of its impact on our family, we eventually became volunteers of Atlanta Free Store. It was so much fun, and the kids learned a lot. Thank you, Tina, for your organization.

All our groceries didn't come from Atlanta Free Store. We also frequented Costco. Those hurried grocery trips became educational field trips, featuring literacy and math scavenger hunts. My kids had all sorts of graphs to record data with the grocery items while skating with their Heelys in the aisles. Oh, the fun of teaching my three children!

There was lots of cooking involved those first years. There was a lot of reading too. All three of my kids read nonstop, which made my teacher heart so happy, my mother heart so proud, and my homeschool-frightened heart relieved. I figured if kids read a lot, half of the schooling was already done.

At the same time I felt relief, my younger self felt jealous. I wish I'd read that much when I was a child. I began reading for pleasure at an old age. Years earlier, I discovered that I have aphantasia. This makes it impossible to see images in my head when I read. Hence why reading wasn't fun for me as a kid.

Because of my aphantasia, I couldn't understand my daughter. When she became a passionate reader, she couldn't help but express the fun she was having.

"I love reading books," she told me. "It's like I'm in a movie! I see it in front of me."

What? Is she crazy? Turns out I'm the crazy one. Sadly, I don't see the character's face, hair, or outfit. I don't see the room or the view the author describes in the story. I see words on a page.

When my parents and sister visited us during those first years, their trips were learning opportunities. Perfect for my kids, who were practicing my language and learning my culture.

My parents are from Catalunya, where homeschooling is unknown. In fact, it is illegal in Spain, though I've read articles where a few Catalan families homeschool under the radar. Some Spanish families have been caught, though after going to court, they've not been punished.

Imagine my parents' surprise. They raised me to be an educated, successful working woman. Then their crazy daughter left their precious Catalan land, migrated to the USA, and married an American man much older than her.

As if that weren't bad enough, their rebel daughter

took their three grandchildren out of the school system to teach them at home.

It was a lot for them to take in, and I knew they would have questions. In preparation, I armed myself with a lot of homeschooling knowledge. When my mom began with her panicky questions, I had my shield ready.

For my mother, all of the questions boiled down to one: *But how do you know they're learning?*

Trust me, you know. There is no need for testing. The children passionately tell you all about what they've learned from a documentary. They share what they heard on a TED Talk or podcast. They want to talk about the book they loved so much. They debate with you about current events in the news. I actually get overwhelmed with all the information they share with me.

My dad, on the other hand, understood homeschooling quite well. He has always undermined school teachers. Besides, his mom homeschooled him. My grandma opted to not enroll my dad in an elementary school during the time of Franco the dictator. Franco's policy obliged all schools—students and teachers—to speak Spanish. Speak your native tongue of Catalan and risk punishment.

This didn't sit well with my grandmother, so she kept my father home. Her love of my father and the Catalan culture led her to send my father to a Catalan teacher. This teacher taught all subjects in Catalan to children of different ages. Because it was illegal to do so, she had to keep her operations out of sight and underground.

My dad loved that teacher and has fond memories

from learning in her very small group environment.

Growing up, I have many memories of my dad looking at the encyclopedia in the living room. He was always curious about something, and he wanted answers. I remember making fun of him because he would literally drop whatever he was doing to feed his hungry mind. At the time, I couldn't understand why my dad wanted to read and learn.

I was a typical kid. I learned in school because I had to. I didn't want to learn outside of school. In fact, when I finished college I was so burned out from studying and passing tests that I yelled out loud on graduation day, "I am done reading books!" Little did I know I would become a bookworm years later and even write a book of my own. Nowadays, I find myself dropping everything to search for whatever my curious mind wants to learn.

Eventually, our educational opportunities came with price tags. After a few years of free or very affordable activities around the city, we wanted to participate in activities that required money. Enrolling the kids in a homeschool running cross country group was inexpensive. Purchasing a Groupon for tree climbing, ice skating, and archery was a bargain. But eventually, the free activities had exposed the kids to their passions. And those passions had a price.

Rock climbing was pricey, as were ice skating and archery lessons. Don't get me wrong. We weren't always out and about. We had plenty of days at home, and my kids are still very good at entertaining themselves at home. They used to spend hours playing with their

PLAYMOBILs, stuffed animals, LEGOs, and playing pretend. They were such a good group together, a wonderful pack of three always playing together. They also enjoyed playing with others. When the neighbors joined in, they had such a blast.

THE CO-OP

We're going to miss the Valentine's Day party!" Afrika said. As my social girl, she was quite worried.

It was February. We'd been homeschooling for just a month. Being so new to the homeschooling world, I wasn't confident. Remember, I became a homeschooling mom without having time to prepare or study what the heck I was going to do.

My daughter didn't care that I was still figuring things out. She was worried that she would miss the school's Valentine's Day party. Her worry made me determined to not be a failure of a mom. So I did what all moms do. I jumped on the computer.

Then I Googled like crazy, trying to find a Valentine's Day homeschool party Afrika could attend. Anything so she wouldn't miss out on what the kids in her old school were doing. Searching the internet like a wild woman, I came across the Atlanta Homeschool Cooperative. The co-op is a group of parents who created a safe environment for kids to take classes once a week, go on field trips, play at the park, and make friends.

We joined the co-op, which was thankfully within walking distance from our house. There, we met new kids and enrolled in classes taught by parents. My children made friends easily, and I made friends too. And these were more than average friendships. They were relationships with real connection. We learned from each other. We shared our troubles and our worries. We shared books to read. When a problem arose, someone would offer suggestions. If someone had already been through the problem in the past, they would share valuable solutions.

Between the co-op, new friends, and playful neighbors of the same age, my kids were busy, and they had plenty of playtime. That's something I noticed. They had so much more playtime than when they were in school. On top of that, they spent an enormous amount of time outdoors in nature.

The co-op introduced me to Amity, Diana, Cayce, Beth, Milena, and many others. These women have been invaluable to my growth as an educator mom. Each has taught me something that made me better.

The co-op also provided my kids with a book club, a science lab, and adventures with various families. Most importantly, the co-op gave me a treasure named Marilyn.

The Co-Op

Marilyn was a beloved teacher in our community. A homeschool veteran with one grown kid already out of college and working, Marilyn was gracious enough to invite my three kids to join a small group she created for her two young children, Javy and Teo. In the comfort of her home, Marilyn taught a class once a week. In return for her generosity, her twins came to my home each week, and I helped them with reading and writing.

Marilyn wasn't an ordinary teacher. She was a fantastic educator. She was very creative with her lessons, was very resourceful, and somehow found time to serve as the director of Peacebuilders Summer Camp and volunteer at El Refugio. I drooled at the chance to help with her classes. I really learned when I helped in her hands-on, engaging classes.

This phenomenal woman taught my kids about United States geography and naturalists. My two youngest eventually lost interest in Marilyn's other classes. Only Jaume joined her US history and science classes, which her husband, a professor from Spelman College, taught.

The classes Marilyn taught were not classroom bound. They came with numerous field trips. We went on a lake excursion with a private educator who taught us all about the lake water while on a boat. We went inside a cave that was so big and beautiful that some people performed weddings in it. We visited the Booth Western Art Museum to see an exhibition of photography by John Muir, an outdoor enthusiast. We went to the Divers Supply Store in Marietta, where you can try scuba diving in their pool. And we visited the George Washington

Carver Museum in Tuskegee, Alabama, where I fell in love with Carver, a smart, eco-friendly man.

Another present from the co-op, Leanna, was a certified Montessori teacher. She started a group at her home called Project Group. Once a month or so, this mom invited kids to her house to educate them about a specific project. The rest of the day, the kids would make a project about the subject they'd just learned about. The group was very successful. Her students wanted more school experience, which led her to open a small school in her home.

We stayed in the Atlanta Homeschool Cooperative for seven years. Around the time my oldest son turned fourteen, he asked to quit attending the co-op classes. Despite dropping the co-op, Jaume kept hanging out with his co-op friends. He just didn't want to join in the activities anymore. The other two kept going until their beloved barn life took over their whole schedule. Once that happened, they eventually quit the homeschool co-op activities as well.

JOHN HOLT

I'm in bed with John Holt!

I laughed at what my friend Beth posted on the Atlanta Homeschool Cooperative FaceBook page.

Is he cheating on me? I wrote, jokingly. *He was in bed with me last night.*

Lots of moms who were reading or had read Holt's books carried on the joke. We'd all been taken by Holt.

Reading his books has been dramatically beneficial for my career in education. I truly believe his work is a must-read if you plan on becoming a teacher or home-schooling your kids. I am so thankful to the woman I met in the lobby of the Performing Arts Center at the West End who suggested I read Holt. She unschooled her three kids and was very pleased with the results.

I read all his books in the right order. It was fascinating to witness Holt's transition from teacher to unschooler. He started by realizing that children were failing in school. Following some investigation, Holt learned the reasons why they were failing. That's what his books are about.

I truly could not have jumped onto the unschooling wagon without Holt. His teachings and discoveries, educational theories, cry for school reform, and call for parents to liberate their children from formal education were instrumental in my move toward unschooling.

After I finished Holt's last book, I felt like I had a PhD in education. I felt empowered and confident, ready to stop teaching my children and see what would unravel. Little did I know my children's interests would lead them to focus on all the subjects I despise, couldn't care less about, or have little knowledge of.

I don't remember learning as much about children's education when I was in college as I did reading John Holt's books. I didn't learn this much when I studied to get my teacher certification in Georgia. I did learn about the famous Montessori, Piaget, Waldorf, and Reggio Emilia, but not John Holt.

I wonder why.

CATALUNYA

Being an immigrant and raising my kids in a foreign land is a tough pill to swallow. I constantly battle with my thoughts.

If we were in Spain, my three-year-old would be in public school by now.

The school food is so much healthier in my country.

What in the world! Little kids say the pledge of allegiance in kindergarten?

I also regularly think about the experiences my children are missing in their lives. They'll never walk across the street to buy a loaf of bread from the local bakery, where the baker knows each family by name.

Of course, I've brought my Catalan culture into our home as much as possible. I've taught my children Catalan culture and celebrated Catalan holidays since they were born. But it's challenging to compete with the

American culture that is so far from Catalunya.

When La Castanyada comes around each year, it's hard to convince the kids to celebrate in the traditional way. They're not interested in roasting chestnuts and eating them alongside sweet potatoes. Because La Castanyada falls on the same day as Halloween, the best holiday in an American kid's life. That's not the only conflict. In Catalunya, January 6 is the most important day of Christmas. In America, kids go to school on that day.

Despite the American calendar clashing with them and despite the fact that I was often the only one celebrating while the rest of America was clueless, I managed to celebrate all the Catalan holidays. I always put a smile on my face and made the best of it. But if I'm brutally honest, I was sad my kids missed the experience of Catalan holiday celebrations.

To this day my kids have neither seen nor experienced Carnaval or Sant Jordi in my homeland. Instead, they have grown up celebrating Sant Jordi at an American chain bookstore. A tradition celebrated on April 23, Sant Jordi is a cherished holiday. That day, Catalunya's streets are flooded with vendors selling books and roses to buy for loved ones.

Our celebration in America is a bit different. We go to Barnes & Noble. Each year on this special day, I purchase four books instead of getting them from the library.

After nineteen years in America, I was given a special surprise. My friend Beth came to our kid's gymnastics class and gave me a rose. I bawled. Nineteen years and one rose. How I long for the Catalan celebrations!

Though we haven't raised our children in Catalunya, Brian and I take them to Barcelona as often as possible. They've gone there for quite a few summers and Christmases, but not as often as I would like. Life and its troubles always seem to come in the way.

My parents have come to visit us numerous times. Also, my sister, my brother and his family, and my cousins have come to spend time with us through the years.

Once the children were out of the school system, I wasn't tied up with work and Brian made enough money to pay for plane tickets. There was no excuse to not go to Catalunya and spend a big chunk of time there.

Exciting as it was for the kids to spend the summer with my family, there was always a problem. Around the two-month mark, they would start to pick up the language more fluently. Then came the hard part.

Leaving.

Each time, it would kill me to return to America, to see my kids ditch the Catalan language and return to American English. But this time would be different. I wanted them to spend longer than two months, plus I wanted them to see the holidays they've always missed during the months of September, October, and January. So we stayed in my country for five months.

The trip began in August 2013. Two of my cousins, Mireia and Júlia, spent the whole summer with us, and we followed them back to our homeland. The kids and I left Atlanta, my husband, and all our pets. While kids in Atlanta go back to school in August, kids are still on vacation in Barcelona. In fact, almost all of Spain is on vacation mode in August.

My dad, a successful and recently retired pediatric surgeon, was completely available to our needs. He became our driver and our unschooling mate. The first trip he took the kids on was to Cadaqués, a gorgeous town on the north coast where my sister-in-law and her parents have a place. That month we visited my uncle Titi and his family at Ripoll, a small town up north on the mountain. While we were there, the town celebrated a Medieval Market. On our journey there, my cousins took us to a secret place only locals know, a beautiful, enchanted small lake with a cascade.

We visited my uncle Salvador and his family at his summer house in l'Ametlla. There, we went on hiking trips and spent hours in their private pool, having a blast with my cousins (my youngest cousin, Marc, is only two years older than Jaume). We also visited my other uncle Joan and his family, who also have a pool. He took us on a sea trip on his small boat. It was a delight to see my kids interact and bond with family members they rarely see.

We then stayed a week in my dad's sailing boat. I love that boat and sailing on the Mediterranean Sea. I hate to brag, but I was the world's luckiest kid, growing up spending summers on a boat sailing to the Balearic Islands. My favorite childhood memory is from summertime. My dad's boat was anchored in Menorca Island, and we had to jump into the water and swim to shore to go grocery shopping.

Playing all day long in the ocean is my fondest sweet

memory, and I'm so glad my kids had the chance to try a small bit of it.

Finally, we stayed a week at a summer vacation village. Named Cala Montjoi near Roses, the village is located at Costa Brava. My uncle Salvador found a great deal that involved my dad.

The village needed a doctor on site for safety reasons. My uncle rounded up several doctors and nurses, including my dad. All of these medical professionals were allowed to spend a week or two at the village at a time. The agreement required these professionals to be on call twenty-four seven, but they got paid for working a few hours and could stay at the village for free.

My family has spent summers there for decades. It has been a family tradition since my sister was one year old. In fact, she learned to walk there. While in Cala Montjoi, my oldest son had the opportunity to try scuba diving with an old friend of mine, and I got quality time with my two nephews.

Throughout our time, my kids got a lot of ocean time, which is important to me. Our Mediterranean is so different from the Atlantic Ocean or the Gulf of Mexico. The fauna and flora are so different, and I wanted my kids to experience it as much as possible.

At the last event in the first month in my country, my mom organized a family dinner. Every summer she reunites her whole family: three brothers and one sister, along with their spouses and children. I have thirteen cousins and most of them have life partners and children. They're invited as well. It's a big party my mom named "The White Supper," because we all must attend wearing white attire.

For the first time ever, we celebrated Afrika and Konji's September birthdays in Catalunya. And for the first time, my kids had the chance to witness La Festa Major.

Early September in Sabadell—the city in which I grew up—is in full celebration-mode. There are concerts everywhere, folklore dancing in every square, activities for young and old. The festivities last all day long for three days straight.

I was ecstatic that my kids finally lived through that festive event. I tried describing it in the past, but it was difficult. La Festa Major is the kind of phenomenon you can only understand if you experience it in person.

They saw Els Castellers, a unique cultural art in which people climb each other to form a tall castle tower. They watched Els Gegants, gigantic puppets that dance through the streets. They went to the traditional fair with bumper cars, roller coasters, and cotton candy. They experienced the famous Correfocs, gawking as pyrotechnicians dressed as devils paraded around the city. During Correfocs, some people watch from afar to be safe. Others cover up with wet clothes and follow closely. It was a blast, an eye-opening experience for the kids!

We visited more family—my dad's sister Angels, my godmother, my cousins, and their children. My dad's brother, Uncle Joaquim, took us hiking at La Mola, a nearby mountain I grew up hiking with my family and on elementary school field trips.

And then, we finally made it to the major event I wanted my kids to witness: The National Day of Catalunya, La Diada.

Held on September 11, this day-long festival celebrates the fall of Barcelona during the war of the Spanish succession in 1714. During this celebration, we commemorate the loss of Catalan institutions and laws. It may seem strange to outsiders, but our national day consists of celebrating our defeat instead of our independence, like other countries happily do.

My country has been peacefully asking to be independent of Spain for years. And on September 11 prior to this particular one, there was a powerful push in the streets. That day, a new, strong independent movement began, leading to this event my kids and I participated in.

With the support of fourteen nongovernmental groups, the ANC (Catalan National Assembly) organized a fascinating event, the Catalan Way. During the event, a 400-kilometer (250-mile) human chain was created in support of Catalan independence from Spain. Across the entire chain, all participants locked hands exactly at 17:14. Hands were held starting from the very south and ending at the very north, symbolizing the unity of Catalan people to achieve national sovereignty.

Goosebumps!

Having my children participate in a Catalan independence peaceful event was enchanting. Having them share such a special moment with their grandparents, who lived through Franco's dictatorship, truly magical.

Celebrating every September 11 in Atlanta was

nothing compared to this particular celebration back home.

Most of these adventures were spent with Iker and Julen, two of my nephews. But mid-September arrived, forcing children to go back to school. That meant it was time for Iker and Julen to return to school. Everyone else—my mom, my brother, and my brother's wife—had to go back to their normal work routine. So my dad, my kids, and I started our own routine, consisting of a tremendous amount of field trips. My favorite was to a vineyard that allowed guests to participate in the process of making wine. We had the opportunity to smash grapes with our feet!

In October, I spent a week at my brother's house. He lives in Sant Joan Despí, a city very close to Barcelona. Staying there made it easier for my kids and me to visit the beautiful and majestic wonders Barcelona has to offer. As an added perk, we got to visit with my two nephews after their school hours.

We went to el Parc Güell, la Sagrada Família, Arc de Triomf, the Chocolate Museum, La Pedrera, la Casa Batlló. You name it, we went there. We were just like tourists.

All those outings came with conversations that led to learning. Though visiting those sites was extremely educational, the most astounding moment was taking my kids to the famous Catalunya Square and repeating what I used to do when I was a child.

Growing up, I would purchase bird food from a street vendor, put some on my palm, and let the pigeons come to me. It's such a lovely activity. Doing this with my children was a gift!

Sant Joan Despí is where Barça, the famous Barcelona soccer team, trains. One day, as we walked around minding our own business, we noticed a big group of people gathering. I asked what they were doing. A man surprised me by saying, "Messi is about to come out. His training is done for the day." Of course, my kids and I joined in. Messi is, after all, the most famous soccer player in the world. We didn't wait long before a black SUV came out. Immediately, everyone started taking pictures, and indeed it was him, Leo Messi, in front of us, for just a moment.

I spent another week in my uncle's house in Ripoll. We visited with my aunt Núria and two of my cousins, Júlia and Mireia, the same cousins with whom we had a blast during summertime in Atlanta.

Ripoll offered us nature, hiking, bike trails, cows, sheep, horses, and a river. When my family left for work and school, we traveled around the cute town. We rented bikes and went on a fascinating trip, visited museums, and hiked the mountain behind my family's house. At night, we had a wonderful bonding family time. Truly magnificent.

And if you think life can't get any better than that, it did. October 31, the day we celebrate La Castanyada and kids in America celebrate Halloween, finally arrived. In my land, surrounded by my culture, my kids finally celebrated La Castanya properly.

My aunt Blanca, a smart, independent, peaceful

woman (some of us are convinced she is an angel) is a dietician. She works catering meals in schools. Aunt Blanca loves to cook and is really good at it. I don't remember if I asked or if she offered, but I'll always remember a workshop she led in her small kitchen. During the workshop, she taught us to make panellets, the round pastry made of sugar and almond, sometimes potato or sweet potato, that we eat on October 31 and November 1 and kids often make in school.

Tots Sants, November 1, is the holiday right after La Castanyada. On this day, we go to the cemetery to visit our dead loved ones. It was nice being able to show my kids where my grandparents are buried. Cemeteries in my city are very different from Atlanta. Some caskets are buried underground, but most are placed in a tomb on a wall, lined up next to and on top of each other.

One of the public libraries in my parents' city offered a free program for school-age kids. Right away I signed my kids up. This program offered literary education, along with some science. Through the program, they started a garden and studied the vegetable according to the right season to grow. At Christmas, all the kids treated us to a wonderful performance. How mystified to see my kids in a play in my city in my language.

Brian, my husband of twelve years at the time, came to visit us. My sister, a hopeless romantic who loves to dramatize everything, found out it was our wedding anniversary, so she made us get married again. She performed a wedding ceremony in my parents' living room. Jaume was the photographer, and my mom baked a cake.

Once Brian arrived, we went on more field trips, climbed more mountains, and investigated more museums. We visited Figueres, where Salvador Dalí's foundation is, savoring his incredible art.

Since Brian loves to hike (just like Afrika), what better place than Catalunya, with its gorgeous mountains? We took him to mountains Montseny and Vall de Núria.

November also brought the birth of one of my cousin's babies. I have so many cousins, and I have missed so many of their weddings and baby arrivals. I missed my cousin Ariadna's wedding after delivering my daughter in Atlanta. I also missed my cousin Pol's wedding, but thankfully I did attend my cousin Georgina's wedding. This time, I had the chance to go to the hospital, congratulate Georgina on her new baby, and meet and hold the new infant.

Thanksgiving was approaching. Although it is not a Catalan or Spanish Holiday, we decided to celebrate it. My kids and I rarely cook a Thanksgiving meal. For years we were invited to the house of Karen, Brian's older sister. She always hosted wonderful Thanksgiving parties with exquisite meals. More recently, we've been alternating Thanksgiving between Karen and Craig, Brian's brother. Since Thanksgiving has never been my holiday I've always followed whatever Brian wanted to do on that particular day. But in my parents' home, I thought it would be a good idea for my kids and me to show my Catalan family what a Thanksgiving meal tasted like.

I loved spending time with my uncles and aunts when they invited me to their home for dinner. It was a joy to have time to catch up with our lives. But not all the time spent in my country was a happy story. We had some crises too.

My sister Mariona, nine years younger than me and twelve years younger than my brother, has Down syndrome. At the time she was going through some anger management difficulties. When her jealousy surged, her anger would develop. Not knowing how to channel it correctly, a crisis was formed.

For some reason, Mariona felt envious of Afrika. This made my sister go through Afrika's belongings until she found her flute. Afrika was taking flute lessons in Atlanta and decided to bring the flute to Catalunya to practice. Unfortunately, my sister damaged it with her anger.

Another upsetting situation was when Mariona was so angry that she yelled, insulted me, and hit me. I hit her back, and my three kids witnessed the whole damn thing! Those crises, in my opinion, are great teachable moments.

My dad has always loved skiing. While my siblings and I were growing up, he always took us skiing for one week. I despise cold weather. I despise snow getting my gloves wet. And I despise skiing down the mountain, trying not to fall or crash into somebody. Regardless of my hatred for the sport, I wanted my kids to have the experience. So in December, right before Christmas break, I took the kids to the Pyrenees.

Thanks to my dad (who booked and paid for everything) and my mom (who asked family members for skiing clothes to borrow), my three kids had an amazing, unforgettable skiing trip. Not only did they travel to Andorra for a phenomenal time with Grandpa, but they also had a private tutor and an outstanding skiing experience.

During the Christmas break, I enrolled my children in L'Obrador, an after-school activity that offered a winter camp. Walking distance from my parents' home, L'Obrador was where children literally learn hands-on woodwork—sawing, nailing, hammering, painting, and building items with wood. My sister went there when she was a young child, as did my cousins and their own children. People in the city can't say enough good things about L'Obrador.

We went on more one-day excursions. We visited the magical and astonishing Montserrat Mountain and had a lesson with my cousin's firefighter husband. He taught us all the dos and don'ts to avoid the dangers of fire, like not throwing water at a grill full of oily fat. And we walked around the traditional La Fira de Santa Llúcia, a group of vendors who sell Christmas garments.

We even watched Els Pastorates performed three times! A deeply-rooted traditional Christmas play, I adore Els Pastorates. My kids do too. We went to see the play at a famous theater in La Faràndula, at the theater in the neighborhood where we were staying, and at the elementary school where my cousin is principal. My cousin even directed the play!

I was mystified of my fabulous, smart, successful cousin Cristina. She's my age. We grew up so close to each other, and she is incredibly creative. She writes, choreographs, and directs Els Pastorets each year. The oldest grade in her school performs the play annually, and I was delighted to see their performance.

Lastly, in January, we celebrated my birthday. But that wasn't the only excitement in January. We got to celebrate in my own country the holiday I most cherish, the holiday on which my kids had to go to school numerous times in the past and learned to celebrate on the weekends or after school hours: Els Reis!

On January 5, the eve of the Three Wise Men, we appreciated their arrival with a parade in the streets. In the parade, you see the three wise men along with their helpers, camels, and presents, as well as the coal they give to naughty children. (Once as a kid I got coal!) For years in Atlanta, we watched the parade on YouTube. How incredible to finally experience the Three Magic Kings face to face.

During these five months in my country, I secretly decided to try radical unschooling. With the excuse of being away from home and visiting family in Catalunya, I felt it was easier to give it a try without being scared. Once I tested the beauty of radical unschooling, there's no way I could go back to homeschooling.

SELLING THE HOUSE

Homeschooling or unschooling can be done with very little money. With free resources like the library, along with some creativity and thinking outside of the box, it can be done with help of family, friends, and neighbors. But with a good budget, you can do so much more.

My kids liked skating, rock climbing, archery, and tree climbing. This left me with no money to go to the movie theater or a restaurant. I needed a budget for the kids' activities and traveling. My kids and I love to travel, and you learn so much visiting other states and countries. I wanted to provide opportunities that weren't cheap. To do that, I needed more resources for my kids' education. This time, free wasn't going to cut it. So we made a drastic decision.

In 2015, we decided to sell the house and move to

a home with a lower mortgage. I wasn't bringing home any income, and I was tired of being broke. My amazing neighbor Alison, who became a very good friend, is a real estate agent. Oh, how fortunate we were to have Alison take us under her wing and help us sell the house.

From January to April we prepared the house. After I decluttered every room, Alison told me exactly what to do to make the house attractive to buyers. She reorganized the rooms, made them look like a million bucks and told the painters what to do. At the same time, we pressure washed the outside. As final touches, Alison let me borrow some of her gorgeous furniture, and we hid some of my unacceptable material. Gorgeous! My friend is a divine interior designer, and thanks to her work, the house looked stunning.

During the week we showed the house to potential buyers, I gave the kids strict rules. No playing with toys. No messes allowed. Only video gaming, TV watching, or book reading. I needed the house to be immaculate. To keep it that way, we spent most of the day outside at a park.

Thankfully, it took only a week to sell the house. Alison is that good. Not only did we make money selling the house, but we also found a house with half the mortgage.

Despite being cheaper, this house was bigger, and it had a very big backyard. There, the kids spent hours riding their bikes, skating, and playing ball. In the big front yard stood a majestic, tall tree. I was adamant we would have a big, strong tree on our property, as Afrika loved climbing trees. Of course, the house also had its quirks (including a horrendous kitchen), but I was willing to put up with them. The price, space, and character were worth it.

We finally had money in the bank and a smaller mortgage. Alison made sure I was on a nice street in a nice neighborhood. She even gave me a few tips to turn the kitchen from ugly to acceptable.

Now that our income matched our bills, we had a budget for our world schooling. But just like every time I plan, God laughed. Once again, my plans went down the drain. We would have to take a rain check on our plans to travel to New York, ski in Vermont, and relax in Hawaii.

THE HORSE YEARS

I felt like a fish out of water every day I was involved in the equestrian world. It began in August of 2015.

Brian was earning more income than usual. Combined with the money we made from selling the house, we could afford one of those pricey summer camps that we never had money for in the past.

Every summer I would ask Afrika, my animal lover and circus admirer, if she wanted to attend a horse-riding or circus camp. In the past, she always said no, but this specific summer, she said yes. She would like to attend a horse-riding summer camp.

Most equestrian schools are far from the city, but we were fortunate to find a barn closer than all the others. Ellenwood Equestrian Center was only a thirty-minute car ride away. I signed up Afrika and Konji for a week of camp. They loved it so much, they went back the following week. Then the next and the next. That summer, they never left horse camp.

Once summer was over, they enrolled in year-round riding classes. Eventually, they became good riders. Being very acquainted with the barn, they even became helpers. In their roles as helpers, they helped the owners on the weekends with birthday parties. They also helped adults who came to ride for a one-time event.

Afrika and Konji loved helping so much that they started pitching in during the week. They fed the horses, cleaned the barn, and got paid to ride two horses, sometimes even three, five times a week. Needless to say, they gained a lot of riding experience. They loved the barn life so much that they happily and eagerly became helpers for the summer camp.

Through their horse riding and helping, they made many friends. Additionally, they learned much about horses and barn life, both the working life and the horse owner's life. Those years brought many lessons—good ones and bad ones, but every lesson was valuable. Some horses became colic, some didn't get along with each other, and some went through vet treatment.

Sometimes camera crews were on site to film a music video, short film, or reality show. Sometimes journalists would come to interview the owners. Other times, photographers would come for photoshoots. There was always something going on there. The barn gave my kids a variety of experiences.

Afrika and Konji were deeply committed to the barn, its horses, their friends, and the competitive horse shows.

Because of their dedication, our traveling plans had to go on pause. We even babysat the barn several times while the owners were away. Well, my kids did. They were the super knowledgeable barn workers. I was just the adult, supervising from the swimming pool.

Frankly, I don't like barns. I have zero desire to ride a horse. I like horses from afar, but I don't want to be close to them, pet them, or feed them. But my kids' adoration for those animals made me hold horses by their reigns once in a while. Hilariously, I even learned how to braid their manes for show and became quite good at it!

For a long time, my kids wanted to own a horse. Of all the kids in the barn, four of their friends had their own horse. Buying a horse scared me. Not the purchase itself, but the monthly expenses. Paying the monthly fee to keep a horse in the barn is pricey, and I was terrified of the vet bill if the horse got some kind of health problem.

Lynn, the barn owner, believed my kids were gaining a lot of experience. She said they were becoming really good riders by riding a variety of horses every day. They were such good riders that some horse owners asked Konji or Afrika to ride their horses on days when they couldn't physically attend the barn.

One of the most talented girls in the barn outgrew her beloved horse, Gracy. Not ready to part with her and wanting her nearby, the girl and her mom came up with an idea. They would lease that beautiful white horse to a barn family. We were one of the families considered.

At the same time, a different mom was looking for

a part-time teacher to help with her daughter's homes-chooling and driving her to the barn. Like a match made in heaven, I found a part-time job taking care of a home-schooled girl who was friends with my kids.

Twice a week my kids and I went to her house, did some homework, and drove to the barn. This job paid me the exact amount it cost to have a horse in the barn, giving me the security I needed to lease Gracy.

It was September 2019, and we were now horse "owners."

CHANGE!

When you least expect it, when you think the kids are settled and following their paths, one of them slices a guillotine through your perfect, well-crafted routine. I remember vividly when Afrika did just that on an early October morning.

It was Tuesday around 11 a.m., one hour before we were supposed to leave the house to head to the barn. I was standing at Afrika's bedroom door. She was sitting on her bed with teary eyes.

"I want to quit horse riding," she said.

My head was spinning, memories of the past few months flashing in front of my eyes. I just found the perfect job to pay for the leasing of this horse. It was the perfect deal for us to "own" this horse.

This behavior of quitting without any warning wasn't new for Afrika. Years ago, she quit violin cold turkey too.

I patiently explained to her that she couldn't repeat the same childish behavior she displayed with Cale, her violin teacher. I encouraged Afrika to be more responsible this time. I suggested she give a two-week notice or at least one week notice to the barn owner. Afrika refused, and I didn't push the issue. Perhaps there was more to the story.

I drove Konji to the barn, because we still had a horse that was our responsibility to ride. Konji told me during the car ride that he also wanted to quit. Actually, he was angry at Afrika. They had agreed to quit together. His sister disregarded their agreement and blindsided him. Thankfully, Konji understood it was his duty to ride that horse that I'd leased until the end of the month.

At the barn, Lynn and Leah, the barn owner and daughter, were surprised Afrika wasn't with us. She never missed any days at the barn. Konji, on the other hand, missed an occasional barn day to stay home and relax.

Lynn and Leah were shocked when I explained the situation to them. The three of us chatted for a while, trying to understand why Afrika wanted to quit. We just couldn't figure it out. Then one of the riding girls told me that Afrika and Konji had been talking all summer long about quitting the barn, but every time, friends convinced them otherwise.

It was the right decision to lease that specific horse from that specific family. The mom and I didn't have a legal contract. We had a friendly agreement. When I explained Afrika and Konji's decision, she completely understood and was very gracious. And my job as a part-time teacher ended around the same time. The other mom's job went through some changes, allowing her to work from home, so she wouldn't need me anymore. Perfect timing.

Eventually, Afrika wrote a farewell email to Lynn, and in November, after leasing a horse for only two short months, we started a new, completely different life.

THE SOCCER PLAYER

Announcing my kids were learning outside of the school system reminded me of announcing we were adopting Konji. A few family members, some friends, and several acquaintances criticized our choice. They were very curious, but they were also scared about our choice. Many told me to my face (and perhaps also behind my back) that they didn't like our choice.

Just like adoption, unschooling required an exhausting amount of explanation to validate our choice. Because simple-minded people have a hard time understanding that life has different paths, they only understand their way of living life. Any other way is not only strange to them, but wrong. Adopting my son and unschooling my three children have been two of the best decisions of my life. These choices have actually improved my life by making it easier, richer, and simply better.

AN UNSCHOOLING EXPERIENCE

Konji, short for Konjinet, was my main factor for switching from homeschooling to unschooling. He's the kind of child that only learns when he wants to learn. He's the reason I read an enormous amount of parenting books. He's the child who taught me to love people like you love a cat—with their personality and independence, without trying to tame or change them, allowing them to approach you when they want to, and being happy with their happiness.

Konji, the youngest of my three, showed signs he was ready to read when he was five years old. So we began homeschooling. He could read easy words like *cat* and *dog*, but when I would ask him to read to me, he would shut down.

I didn't want to interfere with his learning, so I withdrew. I read about and have met some people who learned to read on their own without any instruction. I decided to give it a try. All I did was make literature reachable, available, and attractive.

My house was and still is full of books and children's magazines, so there were literacy opportunities all over the house. As a preschool and kindergarten teacher, I used to place reading material in every learning center the students worked. A classroom shouldn't have literacy only in the library center. Literacy should be found in the play/pretend center, the block center, the science center, and every other area where students spend time. At home, I did the same thing. I've found the best place to put a book or magazine is the kitchen table, where the kids eat their meals.

Back in my days as a kindergarten teacher, parents shared their happiness when their kids started reading. They were so thankful to me, thinking I taught their kids to read. The truth is that I didn't teach them how to read. Not exactly. All I did was offer a variety of literacy opportunities.

In addition to books, there were catalogs, menus, children's songs, audiobooks, daily letters from me, short sentences on the wall, and lots of encouragement. Those kindergartners I adored so much learned to read on their own. I only provided the means. They did the rest. I've found that a child without learning disabilities will learn to read as long as the opportunity to do so exists.

I'm so glad I withdrew from Konji's process as he learned to read. Unlike my other two children and the kindergartners I taught in the past, I didn't teach Konji the famous sight words that are taught in most English-speaking schools. Like magic, my six-year-old boy started reading chapter books.

How do I know he was understanding and comprehending what he was reading? Because he would lie down on his bed, cracking up as he read the My Weird School Daze book series by Dan Gutman. He would laugh so loudly, because he understood what he was reading in those hilarious books. I know he mastered reading comprehension because he read The Chronicles of Narnia by C.S. Lewis and told me all about it. Because he read *Black Beauty* by Anna Sewell and declared it his favorite book. It was obvious to me without the aid of a comprehensive reading school test that Konji was a keen reader.

AN UNSCHOOLING EXPERIENCE

This experiment proved Konji could learn without being taught. Its success encouraged me to give radical unschooling a try. Until then, I was afraid of radically changing our homeschool everyday life—especially with Brian living under the same roof. So on our trip to Catalunya, I informed my three kids to secretly try unschooling once there, just to see if we liked it.

Many people panic and wonder, *But what about math and spelling? How will Konji learn that?* Well, he did. He learned math on his own because he's interested in money. Money taught him to count, add, and subtract. He also learned math while playing video games. He learned how to spell on his own too. In fact, my three kids are all really good at spelling. On the other hand, I'm terrible at spelling in my own language, though I am good at spelling in English.

Some homeschooling families believe that kids who read a lot at a young age will learn to spell without any trouble. While this has been true for my kids, it's not true for everyone. Some of us are just not good at memorizing the correct spelling of a word. No matter how many classes or how much tutoring or testing, spelling is a struggle for some.

Konji didn't magically learn the mechanics of complicated multiplication or division on his own. He asked to be taught. Amity, a very wise friend who was unschooled by her parents, once gave me a piece of advice I've kept close. This advice has really worked for Konji. When Amity was young, she never cared about good penmanship until she realized other kids had better handwriting than her. That's when she started caring. To match her peers, she practiced and practiced until her handwriting was beautiful. I've applied this method with Konji and it's worked wonders.

Around the time Konji was having the time of his life at the horse barn, surrounded by kids of all ages— mostly middle and high schoolers, he asked me to buy him a math book. Why? He wanted to learn the math all the kids were fussing about. I obliged. Now, he works on his math book when he wants to. When he comes across a difficult task, he asks me to teach him. I teach him the way I was taught as a child and the way American kids are taught today. I also show him YouTube videos that explain what he's struggling with. I especially love Math Antics videos.

Basically, Konji learned and is still learning when he wants to learn. When he was younger he wanted to learn to tell time. I happily gathered all the school books I owned that taught how to tell time. But those lessons didn't work. Instead, he would block me out and shut down. I found apps that taught telling time, but the apps didn't work either. I decided to quit teaching him with the school and app methods. Instead, I bought him and his sister each an analog wristwatch. I waited for it to be exactly one o'clock. Then every five minutes, I told them what time it was. Eventually, they figured out the pattern.

Konji's interest lay in geography. He was the cutest kid, sprawled out on the carpet floor of the public library, looking at an atlas almost as big as him. Every time we went to a library or a Barnes & Noble, he would wind up with an atlas in his hands. Due to his passion for maps, he learned all the countries and their capitals, mountains, rivers, population, and flags.

I was amazed at how he retained all this information. As a child in seventh grade, I had to cheat on my seventh-grade geography tests. I simply couldn't remember where things were on the map or the capitals of each country. But you easily remember and memorize the things you are interested in.

Along with his interest in maps surged another. Konji was fascinated with the world's tallest buildings. He loved Burj Khalifa so much that I dreamed of taking him to Dubai while on one of our world schooling trips that were put on hold.

With the tallest buildings interest emerged Konji's architect and design skills. He would often create amazing buildings with blocks, LEGOs, and Minecraft.

Within his geography passion, Konji favored a few countries, making the learning even deeper. He learned a lot about North Korea and Kim Jong-un. His studies taught him so much about government, dictatorship, and the meaning of freedom. It was a joy to see such a young boy learning so much thanks to his attraction to world maps.

I have the cutest memory of my little map-loving boy. While in Catalunya at my parents' house, we were eating lunch at the dining room table. Konji was peeling and eating a clementine when he noticed something. The peel came out as the shape of a continent! He placed it on the table and then continued to carefully peel the fruit, placing the peel pieces on the table. When he was through, he had created the entire world map from a clementine peel. Just precious!

After quitting horse riding and volunteering at the equestrian barn, Konji asked to play soccer. He was very specific on not joining a soccer organization that had parents as coaches. He wanted to join a real soccer academy where they take soccer seriously, because he wanted to be a soccer player. Unfortunately, you had to attend tryouts in May to enter a soccer academy and begin training in August. It was November. We were too late.

One negative of unschooling (or perhaps a teachable moment if you want to be positive) is that we unschoolers don't have a schedule, while the majority of society does, including soccer. The equestrian life has its schedule too, but this new soccer life had a new schedule to learn.

Soon as I found a soccer academy that didn't require tryouts, I signed up Konji. But for some reason, the coach didn't contact me for a long time. Then winter arrived, and soccer season was over. Fortunately, some academies offered winter camps, allowing Konji to start playing soccer at last.

I will always appreciate the coach who didn't get in contact with me when I signed Konji up for his academy. His unresponsiveness, coupled with Konji's eagerness to start playing, pushed me to do more research.

Desperate for a chance for Konji to play soccer, I navigated the internet for soccer training opportunities. Through my research, I found the remarkable Atlanta

AN UNSCHOOLING EXPERIENCE

United Soccer Clinics and their Regional Development School.

Atlanta United FC is a fairly new soccer team. Born in 2015, the club didn't start playing officially until 2017, and they're committed to the development of home-grown players. Only the most exceptional talents within the RDS Program are recommended to join their academy.

This program trains soccer players while still on other soccer teams. They also require their players to pass their tryouts, which are held every season.

That winter, I took Konji to the RDS winter tryouts in downtown Atlanta. Despite having only a little soccer experience, he passed the tryouts. Then he joined the RDS and never left.

In addition to RDS, I found the Inter Atlanta Blues FC winter camp online. Konji really liked what he saw of the camp, so he tried out there as well. He passed their tryouts the following May and joined them in August.

Since Konji started playing soccer at a later age than most and he wants to become a soccer player as his profession, I figured he couldn't afford to waste time during the summer season. After some online searching, we found the perfect summer camp to help Konji catch up on his soccer skills. The Barça Academy in Arizona trains their players three times a day. We sent Konji to Arizona Casa Grande, and he became one lucky kid, spending four wonderful weeks on strict soccer training.

For now, at the age of thirteen, Konji trains twice a week with his soccer club and with RDS. To get more practice, he joins pick-up games around Atlanta on his off days to gain more experience in his game performance.

Away from the soccer field, Konji is practicing reading in Catalan and Spanish and is developing his conversation skills in both. He's also reading the classic book *Lord of the Flies* by William Golding.

Konji actually stopped reading books for a long time and recently asked me to start getting him books again. He reads the monthly magazine we get in the mail, *Upfront* by *The New York Times*. Reading this helps him stay updated on current events, though he already knows about them from watching YouTube.

He's also spent quite a long time watching movies and shows on Netflix. He is now watching documentaries, and *Seaspiracy* on Netflix has really impacted him.

Konji is starting to do the same as his older brother. He shares his knowledge with me, tells me when he's angry about something, and explains all about the mechanics of certain organizations. He talks and debates for endless hours about all the things he reads, watches, hears, and realizes. That's how I know he is learning.

I'm going to try my best to help him reach his goals. Konji has known since a very young age that he doesn't want a job that requires working on a desk in front of the computer from nine to five.

Brian and I agree that if our kids don't want to go to college, we won't push them to do so. Though we're both college graduates, Brian and I are incredibly happy that our kids know who they are and what they want in life. If their passion doesn't lead to college, perfect! If their passion leads to college, we'll try our best to help them get in.

While writing this chapter, I received an email from Atlanta United RDS. One of the coaches has recommended Konji for their showcase. This recommendation doesn't mean Konji will get into their Academy. It does, however, put Konji one step closer to reaching his dream.

In the meantime, I'm learning a lot about the soccer life in order to help him navigate it.

THE AERIALIST

Let's start by taking the elephant out of the room. Yes, her name is Afrika. Yes, with a *k*. When I first fell in love with the name Africa, I had no idea it would cause so many headaches in the future.

I was nine years old. In my new ballet class, a new girl appeared in the changing room. She mentioned that her name was Africa. I couldn't believe that a person's name could come from a place on the map. I thought it was the coolest name ever and fell in love with it instantly.

Since then, I knew if I ever had a daughter, her name would be Africa. How little did I know then how much racism the US has.

As soon as the pregnancy test was positive for my second child, I broke the news to Brian.

"If it's a girl," I said, "I want her name to be Africa. You have nine months to get used to it."

AN UNSCHOOLING EXPERIENCE

I know I sounded mean, but there's a story behind it. My husband and I had a lot of arguments during my first pregnancy. Two of our main wars involved circumcision and the name of our first child. Brian chose the name Jaume, and I didn't like it at all. I'd even had a boyfriend named Jaume, but my husband didn't feel threatened by my past lover.

Brian's father's name was James. He passed away in May when Brian was just becoming an adult. Because my son was born in May (ironically on Mother's Day), Brian liked the idea of naming him James, but in my Catalan language—Jaume. After losing the battle of naming my son, I was determined to name my daughter, and I already knew what her name would be. I would give her the name I'd loved since I was a child.

Announcing that I planned to name my daughter Africa brought turmoil in the US. (In Spain there are more girls named Africa nowadays.) So I decided to find an American baby name book. I wanted to see if I was crazy or if in fact, Africa was in the name book.

Not only was Africa in the name book, but it also gave different ways to spell it. Imagine my surprise when I learned that in America, you can spell names however you want. I had the freedom to switch the *c* for a *k*. The option was alluring. I easily ditched the "correct" spelling and named my daughter *Afrika*.

I love her name so damn much! And once Brian read in the name book that Afrika is of Celtic origin, he was all in.

There are many girls in the US named Virginia,

Georgia, Carolina, Dakota, and Brooklyn. Nowadays, you hear the names Ireland, Asia, America, London, and Paris, all of which you find on a map. Americans are not scandalized by my daughter's name being the name of a continent. They're scandalized because of which continent it is.

Afrika has always been very bright and curious. When I was helping her shower one night, she looked up at me, a question in her three-year-old eyes.

"How come we can pass through water?" she asked.

She showed me the waterfall from the faucet as her hand passed through. She didn't want to know that there are solid and liquid items. She wanted to know why solid objects—human beings—can pass through the liquid ones.

I had no idea how to explain atoms and molecules to a three-year-old. I responded by saying that there is an explanation, but it's so complicated that I would teach it to her after her shower. Afrika didn't let me forget my promise.

Once in her pajamas, she asked the question again. I tried my best to explain the properties of water by showing her child-friendly science videos. Thank goodness for science videos on the internet!

This is the same girl who was a math whiz at an early age. I used to ask math problems during supper time. Once I said, "There were seven potatoes on my plate, and now there are four. How many did I eat?" Jaume, a five-year-old kindergartner at the time, panicked. Afrika, who was only three years old, perked up.

AN UNSCHOOLING EXPERIENCE

"You ate three potatoes," she happily answered.

At a young age, she could do math easily without being taught. It was impressive to watch.

In kindergarten, Afrika was placed in the lowest level reading group at the beginning of the school year. At home, we practiced reading regularly. Every night, we would review the ten sight words the teacher gave us every week for homework. As a result, Afrika flew through each reading level group until arriving at the top one.

Unlike Jaume, Afrika didn't spend her kindergarten year reading easy-level books. She went from reading sentences like *cat is fat* and *pot is hot* to reading a Junie B. Jones chapter book in one night. And she read those books night after night. She read all twenty-seven of Barbara Park's wonderful Junie B. Jones books in no time. She's been an avid reader ever since.

During her kindergarten year, Afrika was tested for the gifted program. When Jaume was in second grade, he was tested too. But he didn't qualify as gifted. I knew that he was a regular smart kid, gifted in other areas of course, but not gifted in academics. I learned during Jaume's second grade year that while he was in class, the teacher wasn't always allowed to teach a lesson and move forward. Any time the gifted kids were in the gifted program or the special education kids were in the special ed program, the regular class was given busy work. This was frustrating, as the gifted kids kept advancing all the while.

When Afrika almost qualified for gifted, the gifted team asked permission to test her again. The second time she did qualify. As a result, she was labeled as *gifted*. I became curious about the situation. Even though Afrika is very intelligent and devours books unlike any child I've seen, she is not a truly gifted child. I think the school system has changed the meaning of *gifted*.

To get answers, I introduced myself to the gifted teachers and asked about their program. From teacher to teacher, we spoke freely and truthfully. The conversation was eye-opening.

During our conversation, I learned that when a gifted kid from another state transfers to Georgia, that child automatically enrolls in Georgia's gifted program. But when gifted students transfer from Georgia to another state, those students must pass the test again to qualify as gifted in their new state. Let me also mention that the amount of money a school receives from the government depends on the number of students enrolled in the special or gifted program. Therefore, the push to test my daughter again.

Around the age of four, Afrika started questioning where her food came from. Every time we ate at the table, she had to know. It was wonderful to get on Google to find answers and images of where broccoli and other foods come from. Her mind was at work! It was such a joy to feed such an inquisitive kid.

But then she asked me a less comfortable question. "Where does steak come from?"

I panicked. I knew where the question would lead. I didn't want her to follow my lead. I quit eating fish when I was young, and I didn't want that for Afrika. I wanted her to continue eating meat. To encourage her to do so, sadly I lied. Please don't judge me. I'm a different person now. But back then, that's what I did. I lied.

The first years Afrika tried to be a vegetarian, I acted like an old-fashioned Catholic not accepting my homosexual child. I had the hardest time accepting it. I had to educate myself in order to have peace with her choice to not eat meat at such a young age.

Eventually, she converted Konji as well. Double punch! Remembering how sad I was about my beloved swimmers being killed and how strong-willed I was about not eating them, I knew I lost the battle with my daughter not wanting to be a carnivore. A radical unschooling mom would have accepted her kids' diet choices without a problem, but I wasn't an unschooler then. So it took me a while.

Once I took Afrika out of school at the age of seven, we homeschooled for a while. It was then that Afrika started mentioning her desire to visit New York.

After we sold the house, I envisioned our days would be filled with learning by planning our trips. I expected the kids would get involved in a project, learning about a state or a country, and then the world. We would go wherever the kids were learning about, and the world would be our school. Then Afrika fell in love with the horse life, putting a pause on traveling.

Besides horse riding, Afrika chose to learn the violin and flute. We bought her a violin and a flute from the wonderful Earthshaking Music store, where their friendly and knowledgeable employees helped me numerous times. I was unfamiliar with the violin and flute world, and they helped me navigate. My only knowledge of music comes from the lessons I took in elementary school. At that time, we learned about classical music from Mozart, Bach, and Vivaldi. Like other students, we also learned to read and write musical notes and to play a few songs on the recorder.

Once Afrika had the flute and violin in her hands, she realized neither were easy. She'd previously taught herself a number of classic songs on the piano. She'd even composed some gorgeous melodies. But she found the flute and violin more difficult than piano.

We'd inherited a piano from Brian's sister Karen. It was a family heirloom, and she was ready to pass it down to another family member. But with these two new instruments, Afrika realized she couldn't learn on her own. She needed a professional instructor.

To get her started, we hired two different teachers who came to our house once a week. Soon, her music skills skyrocketed, and she became really good at both the violin and the flute. Her teachers were impressed and said that at just ten years old, Afrika played at the same level as their high school students.

Years passed, and she suddenly quit violin cold turkey. She mentioned that she was frustrated when playing it. While following the music sheet as she knew to do, her head and heart wanted to play different notes. She wanted to create different melodies.

With such a creative mind, I encouraged her to tell her teacher and to simply have fun with the violin. My encouragement was of no use. She completely closed down and put the violin away for good. She continued studying flute with her private tutor, but this came to an end as well. This time, the teacher had to quit for personal reasons. I haven't heard Afrika play those instruments since.

During Afrika's elementary and middle school years, she didn't do school work at home. She took a few classes with Marilyn, learning geography and about some of the most respected naturalists. She also took a few natural science courses, took a forensic science class, enrolled in drawing classes at the Atlanta Homeschool Cooperative, and participated in a few workshops at the library. All this she did because she wanted to. She was interested in them.

For a long time, she and a friend took private cooking lessons with a chef. But basically, she didn't do any academic learning. However, she read a gigantic amount of books. The librarian was happy, because we brought her numbers up on the library data. This avid reader read all the animal books she could find at the library, memorized everything about those animals, and asked us to test her.

She read series after series of books until Erin Hunter's The Warriors series came into her life. As soon as she discovered those books, she devoured them all. In fact, she loved them so much that she became a fan who joined the Warriors blog clan website, where kids all over the world write and share with each other.

Two books I randomly found at the library became

really beneficial to her—not as learning tools but as therapy tools to help her feel understood. One book was *OCDaniel* by Wesley King, a story about a kid with obsessive-compulsive disorder. I learned as an adult that I have OCD. As a kid, I thought I was crazy, so I kept my obsessions hidden. Because my obsessions aren't extreme, nobody noticed them.

But Afrika couldn't keep hers hidden from me. I recognized them from a mile away. The first time I saw her do something I did at her age, I realized I'd passed my OCD to my daughter. Right away I explained what was happening to her. I told her the name for the disorder and that she's not alone. There are plenty of us out there.

Over the years, Afrika's OCD has manifested very differently than mine. So even though I knew what I was dealing with and was able to coach her through it, some situations I didn't recognize. For example, there was a period of time when she didn't eat or only wanted a very small amount of food to eat. I went mad searching the internet and going to the library for books about eating disorders for Afrika to read. I'd heard so many stories about anorexia and bulimia, and I was ready to nip it in the bud.

Fortunately, an acquaintance shared that her son was in therapy fighting OCD. One of his obsessions was being afraid of choking while eating. I realized then that Afrika wasn't anorexic. Once again, her problem was OCD related. This mom gave me a few tips from her son's therapist. Then I read more about it on the internet. As Afrika and I educated ourselves, we found solutions to these disturbing, unwanted thoughts.

Reading *OCDaniel* really helped her not to solve the problem but to feel understood. I know I would have liked a book about a person as crazy as me.

The other book that benefited Afrika was *A Mango-Shaped Space* by Wendy Mass. This story is about a girl who has synesthesia, the mingling of perceptions whereby a person can see sounds, smell colors, or taste shapes. Afrika has synesthesia too. She sees the black letters in books as colors. People's names have a color in her mind, and numbers have personalities. Mozart, Van Gogh, and Marilyn Monroe had synesthesia. Lady Gaga and Billie Eilish have it as well.

I'll always remember when I learned of her condition. That particular day I was driving my car with my three-year-old girl strapped in her car seat and her brother, two years older, next to her. Out of the blue, she randomly asked, "What color are your letters?"

I had no clue what she was talking about.

"Letter *A* is red and letter *C* is yellow," she explained. "What is yours?"

Just then, Jaume spoke up. "My numbers have colors," he said, "and ten is purple."

Surprise, surprise! He is a synesthete too.

During the autumn of 2019, after quitting the equestrian life Afrika built for four years, she asked to join and get involved with more academic classes.

In the past she took a few classes with the Fulton County Library online system. Those classes are perfect for homeschoolers or busy people since they don't have a schedule and run at their own pace. But Afrika always thought those classes were too easy. She wanted to be in a real, more challenging class.

It was November. As usual, all the available classes had started in August. But I wanted to give her what she wanted. So I begged my friend Marilyn. Along with her husband, Marilyn was teaching a homeschool high school science class. What better place to challenge Afrika than with Marilyn and Gene? That spring, Afrika joined the Atlanta Homeschool Cooperative classes again.

In November before Afrika rejoined the co-op, Cirque du Soleil was in town. As usual, Brian bought tickets for all of us to see the show. Every time they're in Atlanta we go see them. Brian and I are huge Cirque du Soleil fans! Our love for this extraordinary artistic and elegant cirque is one of the very few things we have in common. But Afrika took the meaning of *fan* to a new level.

She's always liked Cirque du Soleil. Since she first saw them when she was three years old, she was hooked. But this last show named "Volta" completely mesmerized Afrika. She was so utterly in love with the performance that she saw it nine times. With her own money and the help of family members and Christmas gifts, this four-teen-year-old was able to pay for eight more tickets!

So when Afrika asked for aerial acrobatic classes, we weren't shocked. On the contrary, it made perfect sense, and I saw it coming. I'd actually offered her classes every now and then in the past, but she always refused them.

From a young age, Afrika was a natural climber. She

climbed every tree she could get her hands on, using her bare hands or the help of ropes. She climbed rock walls, poles, anything.

With such a love for climbing, she loved going to Panola Mountain. Through their tree-climbing program, she became a pro at maneuvering climbing ropes. And she mastered rock climbing at Escalade, thanks to a fantastic and magical rock climbing gym there.

At our new house, I did my best to please Afrika's hanging-in-the-air-from-a-tree needs. To create a cheap copy of the Cirque du Soleil silks, I tied an unused baby wrapper to a small tree in our front yard. Afrika immediately performed impressive moves. This led me to buy her yoga silks on Amazon. She continued with her acrobatic creativity, so I bought her real performing-arts aerial silks.

For two years, Afrika taught herself to use aerial acrobatics silks in our front yard. Day after day, she hung from our enormous, strong tree, twisting and spinning on the silks that my handy dad helped me secure in a safe way. Even after working at the barn all day, Afrika still had the energy to climb those aqua blue aerial silks and perform.

Once Afrika quit horse-riding, her devotion to acrobatics increased. She soon enrolled in classes at Challenge Aerial in Grant Park, where she learned silks, trapeze, and lyra. Going to Challenge Aerial three times a week, she quickly became very good at it. This puzzled her teachers. They were used to new students coming from ballet or gymnastics, but Afrika came from the equestrian world. She'd never even taken dance or gymnastics classes. Yet she moved so naturally.

Those hours working at the barn, carrying hay and water buckets, paid off. Afrika had developed a really strong upper body. And the hours at the barn's pool, playing with friends, choreographing synchronized swimming, and having endless handstand competitions—during which I would yell, "Pointy toes, straight legs, like a ballerina!"—really helped her pretty form.

When the COVID-19 pandemic hit America in March 2020, the world went on lockdown. Afrika used that time at home wisely and thrived. During that time, Brian started working from home, Jaume continued video gaming with his friends online, and Konji alternated screen entertainment with backyard soccer. I was happy to have a break.

Instead of driving kids everywhere—dropping off Afrika at aerial classes, speeding to pick up Konji at soccer practice, and being late to pick up Jaume from work—I enjoyed quiet days, reading on my comfortable swinging chair in the backyard while wearing my favorite garment: a bathing suit.

During our five months of lockdown, Afrika took several free classes from Harvard online. Additionally, she came up with a schedule to keep her athletic skills sharp. Always seeking to improve, she worked on her flexibility and practiced silks in the front yard daily. Since the weather was rainy so often, Afrika was apprehensive of taking her aerial silks outside. To protect her silks, she started practicing aerial moves on the rope that hangs from the tree that we use to bring her silks up and down. She was remarkable on that rope from Lowe's. At the time, she didn't know that rope would become her favorite aerial apparatus.

When June arrived, some places that were on lockdown started to open. The Barça Academy in Arizona opened, and Konji went to get trained during the pandemic. With our masks on, I flew with Konji to Arizona. Together, we witnessed how society was dealing with opening up businesses with all the safety precautions.

Back home, I felt sorry for Afrika. While her little brother was off practicing soccer in Arizona, Challenge Aerial was still on lockdown. I ferociously Googled for circus aerial acrobatic centers that were open. Finally, I found Akrosphere in Alpharetta. Akrosphere opened back up in June and offered summer classes.

As soon as I showed Afrika the Akrosphere website, she fell in love with the idea of taking rope and duo, two classes Challenge Aerial didn't offer. What was supposed to be just a summer experience until Challenge Aerial studio opened up became Afrika's new life.

Today, Afrika is enrolled in Akrosphere year-round. Things are done safely, with students wearing masks and all the pandemic precautions in place during rope, duo, and trapeze classes. And because the coach saw Afrika's talent, he invited her to join the performing circus arts company Akme!

For her fifteenth birthday, we bought her a corde lisse, an aerial rope much pricier than the one from Lowe's she started learning on. For Christmas, we gave her an aerial hoop called a lyra. Afrika is so talented and works really hard every day to become better. I have no doubt she will accomplish her dream of joining a circus.

Being well-rounded, Afrika has contemplated the idea of going to college to study medicine. She is particularly interested in skin diseases and podiatry. But she also wants to go to the National Circus School in Montreal. For now, we're working on both paths.

However, she's currently focusing more on the circus path, because her body is young, strong, fit, and very athletic. At the same time, she's slowly studying high school. She likes learning academic subjects for fun, and she'll need academics if she wants to pursue medicine.

Before the pandemic hit, we were planning to enroll her in Georgia's dual-enrollment program. This allows high school students to take college classes and earn dual credit. In other words, the credits help you graduate high school while earning college credits at the same time. The free program is a fantastic way for homeschoolers to get their feet into the university door.

However, COVID-19 changed that. Instead of dual enrollment at the nearest college, Afrika enrolled in an online high school. There are plenty of free classes on the internet. Khan Academy and Coursera are wonderful websites to learn. But we were looking for an accredited high school that would give Afrika a diploma and a transcript.

When Afrika enrolled in Whitmore Academy High School online, she loved their classes and assignments. She got A after A. I joked with her because I've never been an A student and I never cared to get A's. In fact, the only A I got in school was foreign language English. The only reason I got A's in that was because my parents paid for private English lessons after school, so I was advanced. But my grades in all the other subjects were always B's or C's. Even though Brian and I never expected her to get A's, Afrika was very strict with herself. She expected herself to only get A's. It was important to her to be the smartest.

Because the school keeps parents informed of their students' progress, I noticed that Afrika wasn't sending in homework. The school is self-paced and there's no schedule whatsoever, so she didn't have any due dates. With no due dates, she wasn't pushed to return her completed assignments.

In previous classes Afrika participated in, she always turned in homework minutes before it was due. Somehow she was anxious to send the homework and waited until the last minute. However, she absolutely enjoyed taking tests and passing them with flying colors, especially the free online Harvard classes in which she got an A.

I told Afrika it was okay to receive a B. I explained that mistakes are good, they help you learn. Besides, teachers like to explain things to their students. They want to help their students understand. Despite my talks, Afrika wouldn't budge. She had a fear of making a mistake and an intense need for her homework to be perfect.

Obviously, my daughter is a perfectionist. Perfectionism is a great tool for an acrobatic performer. When she holds another acrobat in the air, everything better be perfect or someone will get hurt. But such perfectionism is also a curse in other areas of her life.

Whitmore is a self-paced school without due dates. Afrika panicked that she wouldn't get an A on her grade. This fear blocked her to the extent that she never sent in her homework. Talking to the wonderfully caring educational director of the school, I learned that Afrika has perfectionist anxiety, a condition OCD people are prone to experience.

In an effort to find a solution that matched the school's philosophy, we came to an agreement. From that day, Afrika would audit the rest of the school year. For the educational director and me, it was important that Afrika not lose her love of learning. We both agreed that it's more important to want to learn than to get grades and credits.

It was heartbreaking to see the effect of anxiety on Afrika. She loves to learn. This anxiety was preventing her from it.

When Afrika found out the school gave her the green light to learn without completing assignments, her face lit up. She is now a sponge, free to soak up all the academics possible on that school's website. The school doesn't test the students. Instead, students have a steady stream of projects and assignments to complete. Because Afrika isn't doing the assignments and there are no tests for her to take, she won't get school credit. But I already have the experience of making a high school transcript. I did it for Jaume, and I know what to do for Afrika's.

She asked me to take care of her education once her

auditing year finishes in August. I'm going to help her find classes on Coursera and Khan Academy, as well as at our public library. All these wonderful courses are free. Since Afrika does really well in college classes online, I'll also continue looking for free classes on edX.org, where universities like Harvard, Berkeley, Georgetown, and Columbia offer courses. Afrika thrives in college classes, so we'll aim for that.

THE WRITER

My firstborn, the surprise baby who stayed with me his first year of life while I worked as a nanny. The one who experienced daycare, elementary school until fourth grade, homeschooled, and later unschooled. Now eighteen years old, he speaks three languages, works as a barista at a local eco-friendly small coffee shop, and is writing a book on his off hours.

Jaume was an A student in school. It made sense for him to have A's in language, reading, writing, Spanish, social studies, and history. But why was my son an A student in math? The kid was clueless at solving math problems!

Well, it turns out you can be an A student at math if the tests focus on one specific area. For example, a test full of only multiplication with two problems at the end that have to be solved using multiplication. Easy. Then, the next test is nothing but division. There are a bunch of division questions on a page and then a few problems at the end that require division for solving them. No variety whatsoever.

Of course the kid was an A student! Like a robot, he could divide and multiply when asked to. But when he came face to face with a real-life math problem, Jaume would go into full-on panic mode. Then the guessing game would start.

"Is it multiplication?" he would ask. "Do I divide?"

He honestly didn't know. And it was a simple problem that required addition. He stressed out when asked questions about time, money, or any life skill taught as a math subject in school. My A student couldn't figure out answers to simple questions.

We arrived at the pool at 12 p.m., and we are now leaving at 4:30 p.m. How many hours have we been at this pool?

Ask Jaume that question and he would give a blank stare.

How very sad that the school labeled my son an A math student when he can't function outside the school classroom when real-life math comes around. Once he was out of the school system and we started homeschooling, I told him to forget the math he learned in school. It was a plus that he knew the mechanics of addition, subtraction, multiplication, and division. However, they were useless if he didn't know when to apply them. I stopped asking him math-related questions and suggested he give math a break.

Math is my favorite school subject. I know a lot of

people are intimidated by or scared of math, and many despise it, but I wasn't going to allow my kids to hate mathematics. I love math so much that my kids once gave me a math problem to solve as my birthday present! To prevent Jaume from hating math, I explained that math is difficult for a lot of people. He just needed a break from it, to completely forget about it.

Imagine my surprise that summer. We were at the public pool, and I was enjoying watching my kids swim and play in the water. Jaume came to me and told me out of the blue, "We've been here for three hours." My teacher heart leaped with hope, and my mom heart filled with pride as I realized my baby could do the math!

Jaume's interests are history and social studies, basically the school subjects I wasn't good at or interested in. When your child has no interest in the subjects you absolutely rock and prefer those subjects you don't get, unschooling gets tricky and challenging.

This is when I learned about things I didn't have any desire to learn. I had no choice. Because fortunately (and exhaustingly), kids will tell you everything they know about whatever subject they love. When their passion is ignited, there won't be a need to test them. Trust me. They'll spill all their knowledge to you.

My first step to satisfy Jaume's cravings for history was to ask around the co-op for advice. Luckily, that year it was a fad to read The Story of the World series by Susan Wise Bauer to your kids. Many moms were reading or had already read it to their children. I borrowed the first book from a friend and gave it to Jaume.

AN UNSCHOOLING EXPERIENCE

"Hey," I told him, "a lot of moms are reading this book to their kids. They say it's a good book to learn history. I don't want to read it. Do you think you can read it alone?"

I've always been truthful with my kids. One thing I learned from a children's therapist is that it's better to be yourself than a fake parent. If I read The Story of the World to Jaume, he would have felt my boredom. By providing him the book, he felt cared for. And he read it. In fact, he liked that book so much he read all four in the series.

The co-op also offered history classes, which Jaume eagerly attended. My history-loving husband carried on many conversations with Jaume during suppertime.

The history of my country is quite long compared to the US. Not only is it long, but it's also thick, complicated, and full of drama. The Catalan history children's books I own only cover a vague part of that history. Needless to say, they were not enough for my young historian.

I was fortunate to meet a fellow Catalan immigrant, a history lover, with no job here in Atlanta. His wife came to the US for a job, and he followed her. Consequently, he was quite bored without any work. I proposed that he teach Jaume the history of Catalunya. He took me up on the offer.

What was supposed to be a short semester (because that's all I could afford money-wise) lasted more than a year. We were sadly very broke and trying to make ends meet. But having my son learn the history of my native land was worth it.

The teacher's name was Hadar. He lived far from us, and it was quite a trip to get to his house. On winter days, I dropped Jaume off at his house and then took the other two kids to the nearby Barnes & Noble, where they devoured books. On summer days, we were allowed to play and swim in the pool at Hadar's apartment complex. It was heaven!

Hadar gave Jaume an enormous amount of homework that required the help of Google. Unfortunately, there aren't many books in Atlanta's public library about my country's history, so the internet was the only tool we had to complete the Catalan history homework. To help Jaume, Brian and I bought Jaume his own computer. His tenth birthday was coming in May, and Google just created Chromebooks. One of the cheapest computers I've seen, it was the perfect present for my responsible, mature ten-year-old.

Another step I took to give Jaume social studies was ordering magazines. We had subscriptions to *Time for Kids*, *The New York Times Upfront*, and others. These magazines were really good at keeping us updated.

Jaume also watched the news on kid-friendly websites and listened to the news on the radio. He's been following current events ever since, and he hasn't stopped learning history since the day I offered him the first book of The Story of the World. History and politics have been a constant in his interests. He regularly attended history classes with Marilyn or teachers from the Atlanta Homeschool Cooperative.

Marilyn, the mother of Jaume's friends Javy and Teo,

is the perfect adult for my son. She is my counterbalance. While I am loud, crazy, and immature, she is serious, mature, and peaceful. While I'm a great improviser, she is a planner. Basically, I have all the attributes that are not a good match for my son. Marilyn has all that I lack. She is a very knowledgeable and responsible rule follower, the perfect role model for Jaume.

Once my politically conservative son described Marilyn as his favorite liberal.

How lucky for my son to have this adult in his life. This wonderful woman educated my son in all the ways that I couldn't. She has also taken him on many family trips around the US.

As much as I love Marilyn and how good she is for my son, her plans and wonderful educational ideas were suffocating me. This put me in a tricky situation. I'd found the perfect role model for my son to learn from, but her extroverted personality and meticulous planning were drowning me.

It turns out that I'm an introvert who gets exhausted by social butterflies like Marilyn. On top of that, my rebellious tendencies make me incapable of planning. I can't plan for the life of me!

Once Jaume turned fourteen, I explained to him that if he wanted to continue taking classes and adventures with Marilyn, that's fine. But I wanted out. I explained that in high school, moms are less involved and adolescents take the reins. I said the same thing to Marilyn and asked her permission to not participate. I told her I wanted Jaume to take control of his education and let me be less involved. I'm so thankful she agreed. I miss spending time with Marilyn, but I'm very busy with my other two kids, and I'm glad Jaume found his path without me. Unschooling comes with difficult decisions like this. But no one said parenting is easy.

Because Jaume liked the science lab at his last school, I subscribed to the Spangler Science Club. This offered Jaume the opportunity to engage in science at home. Each month, a complete kit gets shipped to our home with hands-on experiments and challenges that taught Jaume to think like a scientist. Eventually, the co-op had a science lab. In it, kids dissected a specimen each week. Thanks to Gene, a professor from Spelman, Jaume had a true lab experience, dissecting a brain and other items.

Jaume also found a passion for archery. It all started with one of our trips to Panola Mountain. At Panola Mountain, they offered beginner classes that he took several times. Because Jaume's interest was piqued, I had to find him an archery club where he could take classes. Over time, his skills advanced, and he purchased his own bow and arrows. Sadly, the club closed when the owners retired, forcing us to find another club.

As with the other kids' learning activities, archery wasn't offered close to home. After long consideration, we chose 10 Ring Archery in Woodstock, a forty-five-minute ride on a trafficless, joyous Sunday morning. Unfortunately, his Junior Olympic age group met on Friday evenings. In Atlanta, that translates as "traffic nightmare."

If you're familiar with Atlanta traffic, you may think

driving on the highway every Friday night, full of slowly moving traffic, is a nightmare. But my dear reader, let me reveal something to you. Those Friday evenings sitting in the car, stuck in traffic, were not nightmares. They were a wonderful blessing. We turned on the car radio, listened to the news or an NPR story, learned something new, discussed and debated a current event. Those car rides were Jaume's social studies class. They also gave me an opportunity to learn what he knew. This kid was so intelligent and knowledgeable about politics that it was becoming harder and harder for me to pretend to be a smart, mature adult.

When Jaume turned fourteen, I encouraged him to get a job. He tried. But none of the few companies that will hire fourteen-year-olds had any jobs available. Fortunately, his uncle Craig, Brian's older brother, hired him during the summer for a miscellaneous errands position. He cut weeds, cleaned windows, shredded documents, and babysat their puppy. Thanks to Craig, who paid Jaume a very generous income, Jaume was able to buy his own computer. He saved up, bought computer parts, and built his own PC all by himself. I was surprised and pleased to witness unschooling at its finest.

Unschooling can be easy but it also has its difficult moments. One such challenge involved taking Jaume to a gun store, where you can practice shooting, and to a gun show. I was so uncomfortable in those places, because I despise guns. (I'm afraid of real weapons that kill, but I think plastic play guns and air-soft guns are a lot of fun.) While I hate guns, my son likes them. So much that I wanted him to get his gun experience. Just like any other lesson, it was my duty to provide it.

Another difficult experience involved fishing. Jaume enjoys it. In order to understand this catastrophic situation, you must remember that I decided to stop eating fish at a very young age. Fish is a big part of the diet in my culture. People in Catalunya love to eat fish, my mom especially. But I grew up near the ocean and spent every summer in it, loving everything about it. I couldn't stand eating my swimming friends and seeing them dead at the dinner table. I swallowed my own preference to serve my son. This past Christmas, we bought Jaume a fishing rod! And yet, I wish he wouldn't kill fish.

Unschooling doesn't always go the way you want. I failed at persuading Jaume to fix the shed we have in the backyard. Actually, it's more than a shed. It's a very cute, very small house with a small bathroom and a sink. It looks like it used to be the maid's house back in the day. It's so run down and falling to pieces that we use it to store bikes and lawn items. I would have loved my kids to immerse themselves in renovating the small house. Such a project teaches so many lessons. But none of the kids were interested, even though I told them it could be their own space if they fixed it.

Nowadays my highly sensitive, introverted child has reached adulthood. He has a wonderful group of video gamer friends, a girlfriend, and a high school diploma. He's holding down a job, while writing a fiction novel.

I remember vividly when Jaume was about eight or nine years old. We were both in the kitchen in front of the fridge, and I did something crazy, as I do constantly. Jaume shook his head desperately and said, "One day I'll write a book about what it's like growing up with you." I laughed so hard, because I couldn't imagine what it must be like to be a mature, responsible, quiet, and serious kid being raised by an enthusiastic, wild woman like me.

He's undoubtedly a writer and an editor. I've seen those skills in him for a while now. I always imagined he would write speeches for politicians, opinionated political editorials, or articles for a history magazine. But the day he told me he had a world in his head and it came to life when he slept and dreamed, I knew I had to support him while writing his novel.

I made Jaume's high school transcript in case he needs it one day in the future. I was amazed at how easy it was to put down on paper every subject he's studied, because he learned and had been learning nonstop.

Several times in the past four years I asked if he wanted to attend high school. The answer was always no. I told him as long as he read a lot of books and magazines, watched documentaries, followed the news, volunteered in organizations, and participated in Marilyn's classes, he would be fine. Well, I'm pleased to say his high school transcript is more than just fine. It's fabulous. Definitely better than mine or my husband's.

Great as his transcript was, there was one little important subject missing. Even though he can function in the world with his math knowledge, I couldn't in good conscience write in Jaume's high school transcript that he studied math. To remedy this, I found a good online high school class called Practical Math. I told Jaume it would be beneficial because it teaches the math needed to be a responsible and successful adult. Also, I didn't want to lie on his transcript.

As I write this, he still doesn't have his driving license. He's not in a hurry to get it. He does, however, have his driving permit. Even though he didn't want to learn how to drive, I pushed him to do so, especially since Atlanta isn't an easy city to travel in using public transportation. Atlanta public transportation is very different from New York, London, or Barcelona. In those cities, trains and buses come by very often and offer a lot of route options. Sadly, it's not that way in Atlanta.

I chose to hire a driving instructor for Jaume and his sister, Afrika. My husband didn't want to teach them, and I'm definitely not a good choice of driving teacher. I wish I could have taught them, but I'm a very bad example of a driver. Having a good teacher is vital, as driving is more than a serious matter. Done poorly, it can be deadly.

Once he learned how to drive with the driver educator, Jaume started practicing with me. Dear readers, it is incredibly scary to be in the passenger seat when your seventeen-year-old boy is driving. I do not like it. How do American parents do it?

That said, if you're brave enough to teach your kid to drive, you're definitely capable of homeschooling or unschooling them.

PETS

Having pets has been very beneficial to my kids' education. These wonderful creatures have given us companionship and taught us numerous lessons. It is true, though, that life without pets makes it easier to travel.

I was blessed to grow up with pets around me. My husband loves dogs, and I love cats. Our first pet together as a family was my black and white cat. This handsome, long-hair male cat witnessed the arrival of my three kids and saw all our future pets come and go, passing away just last year of old age.

This cat taught us about eye injury, cat rivalry, spraying, and peeing in the wrong places. In his older age, he taught us that cats eventually stop grooming and scratching their nails. When this happens, their nails grow so long that they reach the inside paws, causing injury.

AN UNSCHOOLING EXPERIENCE

Our first dog was adopted while I was pregnant with Jaume. Sierra was an orange and light brown, fluffy, gorgeous mutt with some chow in her. She also saw my three kids' arrival, but sadly, she didn't stay around to see them grow.

Unfortunately, Sierra loved to escape. She found ways to leave the backyard to go on adventures, from which she would always return. To keep her from escaping, we put all kinds of traps in her favorite escape routes in the backyard. Then she escaped out the front.

When Brian was working in Afghanistan, I was opening the gate to take the garbage to the curve for the city to pick up. Sierra sped by me, sliding between my leg and the gate door. She was gone in an instant. My husband's dog, the dog he adored, never came back. We went to several dog pounds and shelters to find her. No luck. Sierra's disastrous escape taught us the deep pain of not having closure.

Our second cat came from the vet. I wasn't looking for another cat. I went to the vet for my cat's eye problem and left the building with a new kitten. My excuse for the new cat? Jaume, only a toddler at the time, needed a cat of his own. Ross was a very adventurous grey tabby, but he didn't last long. After a short time in our family, he was poisoned by the neighbors, who were sick and tired of him.

Our third cat, Eve, was a sweet, grey tabby that came from the same vet. She was a good companion to my kids, who were four and one at the time. Eve spent many years with us, occasionally coming home with a present.

When she died suddenly in our kitchen, she was an old cat that had lived a good life. One moment she was alive, walking around. The next, she was dead on the kitchen floor.

Our second dog, Kenya, was brought home by me, impromptu. One April day, I was in my kindergarten class, ending the school day. When one of the moms arrived to pick up her daughter, she was carrying a black, fluffy cuteness of a puppy. That puppy looked like a gorgeous, black teddy bear. I had to have it!

The mom told me her neighbor's dog had puppies and there were more available. Without thinking, I got my two kids in the car after work and went straight to adopt this precious mutt that also had some chow in her. When I arrived home with Kenya, Brian was furious. Fast-forward a few months, and Kenya and Brian were inseparable.

Kenya is such a great family dog that always accepts new pets coming into our family. When Sierra ran away that unfortunate day, Kenya followed her. Thank goodness she returned home safe and sound. Kenya taught us that a dog can be allergic to flea bites. My first cat had fleas once, and he did not have any reaction. Kenya did. She started to lose hair, her skin looked horrible, and she was incredibly itchy. Through that experience, we learned a lot about fleas—what treatment does and doesn't work. Presently, we're learning the troubles of aging on dogs, as our beloved Kenya is losing her sight and hearing.

When Afrika was about to turn five, she asked for

a cat for her September birthday. That August, a cute white kitty appeared in our street. We fed her to befriend her, and she quickly became our cat. Now we had three cats and two dogs under the same roof.

That cat, which was nicknamed White Kitty, was the perfect pet for my cat-loving daughter. White Kitty loved being Afrika's baby. She loved being pampered and enjoyed cuddling and being held—the perfect companion for a five-year-old.

Unfortunately, she also loved going outdoors. Being a wild cat, she paid the consequences of a harsh life in the streets. That lovely, cuddly cat was murdered by another wild animal. One early morning, a neighbor knocked on our door and said she thought our cat was dead in her front yard. Indeed, White Kitty was dead. My daughter's cat had a hole in her chest, where it looked like another wild animal bit her.

We normally take our deceased pets to the vet to be cremated, but this cat had a different goodbye. My sweet neighbor Derek, Alison's husband, built a tomb and dug a deep hole in our backyard. We buried our sweet, wild White Kitty, then had dinner together to celebrate her life.

At one point, we had two mice. That took our pet count to seven animals in the house at one time. We quickly learned that mice are not good pets if you like to cuddle. Later, we learned that rats are so much better.

Our first rat came to us at the perfect time. We'd just returned from Spain, where my daughter had to part with her beloved Spanish gerbil Rania. Afrika can't live without a pet, so she received a gerbil in Spain that she took care of for the five months we were there. She knew that when it was time to return to the US, she would have to pass Rania to a family member.

One lovely afternoon while we were playing in our backyard, our neighbor Alison suddenly yelled across her back porch.

"Hey!" she said. "Do you guys want a rat? Somebody in the neighborhood posted on social media that her daughter was allergic to their rat and they needed to find the rat a new home."

My daughter and my neighbor both love to rescue animals. Frankly, I do too. We said we were interested, and Alison contacted the family in the neighborhood. Soon after, we were first-time rat owners. Sanderson came with a cage, food, all the necessary gadgets, and age.

The first time I saw the rat up close, I thought she was very ugly—especially her snake-looking tail. But soon enough, we were all in love with that old, cream-colored female rat. Sanderson brought plenty of lessons to our lives. We learned how smart, clean, and social rats are. We learned that many of the myths you hear about rats aren't true. And we discovered the HeroRATs from the APOPO organization.

Rats are so smart that they can detect landmines and find other explosives. When trained, they save lives. The HeroRATs are not only trained for landmine detection, but also to detect tuberculosis, which they do in Africa and Asia. We studied the history of rats and their breeds, and we experienced the valuable lesson of how a rat recovers from a stroke and gets diagnosed with a tumor.

One day, Sanderson wasn't showing her usual abilities to climb everywhere and to eat. After some Googling, we determined that she had a stroke. It was up to us to nurse her back to health. Immediately, we became vet nurses, feeding the old rat smooshed food and helping her get water in her system. Sanderson slowly recovered, only to display a tumor a few months later.

According to the vet and the internet, tumors are very frequent in rats. We enjoyed Sanderson for quite a while after the tumor arrived. She lasted a long time as that big lump grew bigger. Despite the tumor, she was happy and joyful.

The vet suggested coming to his office once the tumor impeded the quality of Sanderson's life. When you have a pet you love so very much and you spend days playing with that pet, you notice when things change. You know when it's time to go to the vet. We did.

On the sad day we humanely put Sanderson to sleep, we cried a lot. How bizarre that we loved that little creature so much! How odd that we put a rat to sleep the most humane way possible, while others kill rats with poisons or horrible traps every day.

We loved having a rat as a pet so much that we bought a new one around Valentine's Day. She was appropriately named Valentine. This beautiful white and grey rat also brought our family a bunch of joy, love, fun, and inevitably, another tumor.

Since the age of seven, Afrika had been asking for

a dog. Her love and passion for animals have constantly transitioned over the years. It started with cats and then dogs. Soon, it moved on to rodents, and then horses. Afrika read all the dog books the public library offered, memorizing the breeds, along with facts and characteristics about each breed. She loaded herself with so much canine knowledge that by the time her tenth birthday arrived (a special birthday in our family), I couldn't deny her the experience of owning a dog.

Brian and I had already trained two puppies, and we didn't look forward to going through that process again. On the other hand, Afrika had never had the experience of raising a puppy. And adopting a puppy would be easier than bringing an adult dog home to share the house with Kenya and the cats.

So we went to the Humane Society in Atlanta, where we'd spent numerous hours in the past interacting with puppies, dogs, and cats. This time, we were going to take a puppy home. Beautiful, white and creamy Sadie was the chosen mutt.

Sadie's first year in our home was unremarkable. Lamentably, life took a turn for the worse.

Sadie was the sweetest dog with our two foster care kids, living in the house without harming them at all.

First, we babysat a sweet newborn for the State. He was removed from his family after his skull had been fractured by one of the parents. Additionally, he had multiple lesions on his little arms and legs. Then we took care of a three-year-old girl who wouldn't talk. She was very depressed because she missed her mom, an addict who had to go to rehab in order to get her daughter back. My daughter's dog was so gentle with those two kids that we still can't comprehend what happened next.

My dad and my youngest nephew, Julen, traveled from Barcelona to Atlanta to spend the summer with us. Sadie, while being patted by Julen and supervised by me, became an unrecognizable, aggressive animal. Suddenly, this sweet dog became full of anger, biting my nephew on the chest. Mortifying!

My dad suggested that we not put the dog to sleep based on the attack. So we didn't. Instead, we hired a private trainer. Sadie then aggressively attacked Winter the cat, Kenya the dog, and my old cat. We still didn't want to put Sadie to sleep, but she made life miserable. We were no longer relaxed and carefree at home. Instead, we were constantly keeping Sadie separated from the rest of the pets and guests.

Sadly, the training didn't work. Even after the training, Sadie would instantly switch from our good, sweet dog to an unrecognizable, angry wild beast. We didn't have the guts to put our daughter's beloved dog down. Something bigger and more disastrous had to happen.

My hand.

Thank God it was my hand and not any of my kids. On a cold winter day before my fortieth birthday, my right hand was tortured by Sadie's strong mouth. Crying from pain and sadness from what I was about to do, I took her to the vet. Seeing my hand and my crying face, they euthanized Sadie while I whispered in her ear, "I'm sorry, I'm sorry."

My poor daughter—lover of all animals, vegetarian by choice because she doesn't want animals to be killed, had her dog killed by her parents.

Every cloud has a silver lining. At least I choose to believe it does. Sometimes we don't see that silver lining, but I choose to believe it's there, somewhere behind those dark clouds.

After the death of Sadie, I didn't want any more dogs in our home (besides Kenya of course). I was afraid when dogs barked at each other at the park. I was terrified when people let their unleashed dog roam the park, river, or beach, not following the law that says it's illegal for dogs to be unleashed in a public place. I was petrified when strangers let their two dogs sniff each other. After the attack from Sadie, I constantly expected another attack.

Knowing that we would not adopt a dog again, Afrika asked if we could adopt a guinea pig. That's how Saïd came to our family. We transformed Sadie's giant, empty dog crate from something full of sad memories to a guinea pig palace. This new animal kept Afrika occupied, as she learned everything necessary to care for a guinea pig properly.

Afrika quickly learned that guinea pigs poop so much you have to clean their cage every single day. Did you know these rodents poop so much that in Peru, some villages use guinea pig poop as a source of renewable energy that powers the entire town? That's a lot of poop!

Time passed. I started feeling confident that if we ever got another dog, it would be small. I needed to know that in case of an emergency, I had control over the dog. I had to be stronger than the dog. And the dog had to get along with Kenya.

Even this could be a problem. After all, Sadie was brought home as a puppy. She met Kenya while in her puppy stage, and they got along well for a year. Then the second year was a terrible struggle. But I was willing to take a risk for my animal-loving daughter.

Afrika researched all over the internet and found websites that offered small dogs to rescue. I agreed to only adopt a small dog that would get along with Kenya. Two times we met with different foster families and provided a safe meeting for both dogs. Both times, it didn't work out. Frankly, I was relieved. I wasn't in a hurry to invite another dog into our family.

Meanwhile, one of the oldest helpers at the barn found an abandoned dog on the side of the road while driving home in the rain. She brought the dog to the barn and began asking for someone to adopt her. Gratefully, one of the horse-riding families gave it a try. When my kids told me this story, I was happy I wasn't asked.

More time passed. February arrived. My dad came to celebrate his seventieth birthday with us, when I received a text from Leah, the barn owner's daughter and riding instructor. She asked me to consider adopting the puppy that was found on the road.

Apparently, things didn't work out with the first family who gave it a try. So then Leah, an animal lover and owner of several dogs, also gave it a shot. She explained that the dog was incredibly sweet. She just wanted company, which Leah couldn't provide since she was so busy at the barn.

Leah even tried to persuade me by mentioning our family situation. She said Afrika was very sad since her dad left for Afghanistan. A new dog—this dog—would keep her company. I also knew that the same dad who was currently in Afghanistan would kill me if I brought another street dog home.

Honestly, I didn't want that dog. But I couldn't say no. (I learned to say no much later in life.) So instead, I texted back, *I don't want another dog. I can only say yes if my dog accepts her. I will give it a try but if my dog doesn't welcome her, I will have to return her.*

I was convinced Kenya and the new dog wouldn't be a good match, just like the past dogs. But I was going to let Afrika see for herself that the dogs didn't like each other. That way I wouldn't be the villain. I didn't even bother telling Brian or Jaume, because I was sure the dog would be returned.

My dad and I drove to the barn to pick up the kids, and I parked. While waiting for the kids, I saw an ugly white and black dog get passed into my daughter's arms. Oh, my! How ugly that little thing was. My dad, who is not a pet lover, exasperatedly complained.

"Why are you complicating your life?" he asked.

I shushed him. "Shhh! Don't worry," I said. "The dogs will meet, it's not going to work, and Afrika will understand we can't keep this dog. We'll return this puppy tomorrow. It's just one night."

The joke was on me.

AN UNSCHOOLING EXPERIENCE

I dropped Afrika and the new doggy off at the park near our house. Then I drove home to collect Kenya and take her to meet the new dog at the park.

Afrika and I walked the dogs side by side. No problem.

We stopped walking and allowed the dogs to meet. No problem.

We sat down and waited for a problem. No problem.

We went home, as I secretly hoped the two dogs wouldn't get along on Kenya's property. Again, NO PROBLEM.

As soon as the dog entered the house, she ran toward Afrika's room and jumped on the bed

"This dog is great!" Afrika yelled. "She already knows to get on my bed!"

Afrika's definition of paradise is sleeping in a bed full of cats and dogs. At the same time, I'd never seen Jaume so angry. He was completely clueless that we were bringing a dog home, and he didn't want another one.

This dog, which Afrika named Jazz, is the perfect companion for her. A match made in heaven. The silver lining we sometimes get to witness. The perfect loyal best friend Afrika needed.

Nowadays, we're down to only one cat. Winter, a grey tabby from the streets, came to us on a winter day. A neighbor persuaded us to adopt this street cat that was roaming around the neighborhood. I explained that I was incredibly busy and beyond overwhelmed with my new role as the foster mom of an injured infant. But the neighbor wasn't deterred. Rather, she was so warmed up by the fact that we were foster parents that she offered to pay for the vet visits.

This cat took longer to lure into our home. Afrika used her magical cat whispering to attract the cat to her room, and the neighbor and Afrika took care of the rest. This sweet cat spent a whole year in Afrika's room, never roaming the house, only stepping out of Afrika's room to go out in the streets.

Very slowly, Winter has opened up to us. She now sleeps on my bed and meows at me when she wants to cuddle. This cat has taught us the beauty of patient work. We have learned how powerful patience is when caring for a rescued, untrusting animal.

SOCIALIZING

Ha! Those worrisome people who don't home-school used to drive me nuts. Now they just crack me up. I swear with all my sincerity, this makes me laugh.

Socialization starts at home. Socialization is the process that allows a person to learn values, language, culture, behavior, and social skills so that person can function in a community. So what better way to actively learn and practice in the community than be contained in a school building?

You'll find plenty of articles explaining that kids are actually better socialized out of school. In public school, children spend five days a week with peers of the same-age. Being homeschooled or unschooled is like summer-time, winter break, and spring break all combined in one.

Your children get to meet, hang out, and befriend kids of all ages, while growing relationships with the adults in their lives.

Homeschooled kids not only have more opportunities for socialization, but they also have a larger diversity in that socialization with people of all ages and a variety of settings.

The fact that public school children are socialized with mostly same-age kids and few adults made me arrive at the conclusion that homeschool kids are actually better socialized than public school kids. Therefore, it's time we unschoolers and homeschoolers start turning the question around. It's time for us to ask the parents who choose to send their offspring to school:

But what will you do to socialize them?

THE HUSBAND

I've been very lucky to have my dear husband, Brian, who has been on board with all the changes our kids' education has gone through over the years. He gave me the full lead on decisions regarding our kids' educational paths. That I have a degree in education and was a teacher when Brian first met me gave him confidence in what I did and continue to do with our little ones.

He once told me the sentence he fears the most from me starts: "Brian, I've been thinking . . .".

Yes, these words caused us to adopt a child from Ethiopia. They led me to quit my job, which led to our family struggling with only one income. The short phrase brought on so much. Taking the kids to Mexico to spend the whole summer working in a rural school. Returning with the kids home to Barcelona to de-Americanize them. Jumping into foster care. You name it, those words led to it. I've come up with a lot of crazy ideas that scared Brian at first, but now he's glad for all of them. He regrets none of our experiences and even likes when I tell him, "Brian, I've been thinking . . .".

Taking the kids out of the school system was not only a crazy idea to him, but also to me. I didn't want to do it, but I had to. Thankfully, he agreed.

Not all partners are on board when one parent wants to homeschool. Not all partners who are on board with homeschooling agree on the specifics on how to home-school the kids. Such differences cause many couples a lot of marital problems. Sincerely, I've been blessed with my husband trusting me.

I'm not the only crazy one in this relationship though. At the end of 2010, Brian told me he found a job in Afghanistan. At the time, my three kids were seven, five, and three years old. The youngest had just arrived in America and was slowly getting acquainted. Not an easy time for our family. But my husband found a job as a private contractor that would pay an income I didn't know was possible. The only downside was that the job was across the ocean, 9,000 miles away from home. But we would finally be able to pay the debt we were in and build up some savings for those rainy days that seem to always be around the corner. Believe me when I say lots of rainy days came, because they did!

How could we turn down the opportunity?

Many women struggled to understand our decision. Concerned, they asked me, "You let him go?"

I wonder what they mean by the word *let*. I'm not my

husband's boss, and I sure wouldn't like it if he bossed me. Who was I to not let him go?

The same thing happened when I took the kids to Catalunya for five months without Brian. Some people were amazed. They couldn't understand.

"Your husband is okay with it?" they all seemed to ask. *Yes.* Our marriage would not be okay if Brian didn't let me be me and if I didn't let him be him. We love each other, but we are very independent people.

When he mentioned going to Afghanistan, I was supportive. I envied his future adventure and wished the tables were turned. Since I couldn't travel with him, I focused on the large amount of money that would be in our bank account. Initially, it was difficult adjusting to not having Brian at home every night, but we got used to it, and it was worth it.

When he came home to visit, we had wonderful adventures. Because now, we had the means to do them. We could eat out at restaurants, go snow tubing at Stone Mountain, and take trips to Chattanooga, the Georgia islands, and the beaches at the Gulf of Mexico and Miami. We went to Cirque du Soleil shows, and my very favorite—a family trip to Mexico to swim with dolphins on Christmas day!

Though I enjoy being with my kids, I like and need alone time. That's why I used my husband's love for mountains and camping to have him take the kids on trips without me. Brian took them camping to all state parks within a two-hour drive of Atlanta. Of these parks, their favorites were Fort Yargo and Fort Mountain.

AN UNSCHOOLING EXPERIENCE

While camping, everyone won. The kids got quality time with their dad and a great nature adventure, and I soaked in the peace and quiet of an empty home. Oh, glorious, calm, cocooning days! Those were my recharging days. I didn't come out of the house for anything, not even to talk to my dear neighbor friend. I desperately needed quiet time.

My husband participated in our kids' education in the areas I couldn't. He provided economically so the kids could enroll in their beloved activities. He took the kids camping, which Afrika absolutely loved. He had and still has endless conversations about history and politics with Jaume. And now, he practices soccer with Konji.

The most important task Brian took in the kids' upbringing was reading aloud to the kids every day. As an educator, I know the importance of reading aloud to children, but I absolutely dislike being the one doing the reading. When Jaume was an infant, I explained to Brian how important it was that he read to him every night. Happily, he read to every child every night until they could read on their own.

Once the kids were reading on their own and enjoying it, Brian stopped reading to the kids. But years later, when we started unschooling, I noticed the kids weren't reading any of the classics. So I asked Brian to read *Oliver Twist* aloud after supper. It was such a success that they continued reading other classics. Even my dad got in on the action. When he visited, he read *Heidi* to the kids in Catalan.

Unschooling can be difficult and draining when you

don't like doing what the kids need or want. It is definitely important to find someone to help you.

THE FINAL LINE

Every homeschool family has a story about why they chose their particular path.

Some decide to homeschool because their child was problematic in school. Some choose to homeschool because their kid was bullied or diagnosed with hyperactivity. Some choose this path because they were bored as children when they were in school, and they want something different for their kids. Others homeschool because they want their religion to be the main focus on their kid's education.

My story was a series of unfortunate—or rather, fortunate—events. I came to America looking for adventure, and I got it. Becoming an unschooling mom is like being a teacher, special-ed teacher, full-time nanny, researcher, therapist, manager, and more. The list goes on and on, and I am so glad I get to do them all!

AN UNSCHOOLING EXPERIENCE

I loved being a nanny before I became a mom. Those years working as a nanny were fantastic, and I was living the life. I loved those kids so much. I cherished spending summertime with them, picking them up from school and doing homework, getting snacks, and driving them to and from sports practices and games. Those years helped shape me into the mom I am today.

My grandmother once told me that when my dad was an infant, she wanted to talk to him. At that time—1949, it was a tradition to not talk to your infants. For my grandmother, it came naturally to talk to her firstborn. So she ignored that tradition and followed her instinct. Now we know how beneficial it is for babies to be talked to regularly.

Are there other instincts we're ignoring? Other things we know would be good for our children, but society tells us not to do them? Let's change that. Let's follow our guts and our instincts when it comes to raising our children. Let's ignore what's normal. After all, *normal* might change in the future.

I ignored my gut that told me it was strange to put our five-year-olds in school to get educated by a teacher. I felt sad. I didn't like saying goodbye to my son on his first day of kindergarten. But I ignored my inner voice and shoved it down, telling myself to stop being a weirdo. I convinced myself that it was normal to place kids in school and go to work. That's how the system works! Plus, I had my own kindergarten class to take care of.

Dear readers, if your gut is telling you to not send your children to school—if you feel your gut telling you to let your children direct their own learning and that doing so means you still carry the wisdom of your ancestors within you, you're not a weirdo. Unschooling is easy and worth it. You can do it.

If you're doubting whether to put your kid in school, please give unschooling a try. Try it for a year. Live like it's summer break all year round. Allow your kids to interact with life however they want. If your children want to play in a muddy puddle, let them. Just be prepared with towels in your car and a change of clothes in your bag. And if they know how, make them do the laundry after that muddy experience. But please, don't stop them from engaging with that puddle. It may look like a mess, but it leads to learning.

Considering unschooling? I hope this book encourages you and inspires you to reach a decision. If you want to try it but feel a little scared to venture into new territory, here's a simple map you may need: Live every day like you're on vacation.

Afraid your kids will do nothing? That's impossible. Doing *nothing* is doing *something*. Trust me. One day you'll be at the beach relaxing on the sand, enjoying the view of the stunningly clear water of the Gulf of Mexico. Then your almost eighteen-year-old will surprise you with some kind of scientific knowledge that is beyond your forty-three-year-old college-graduate mind.

"Hey guys," Jaume said, "when you lie down and look at the sky, you can see clumps of protein in your eyes."

Um, what?

AN UNSCHOOLING EXPERIENCE

Such insight is a regular occurrence.

I have two more kids to raise for now, but reaching the finish line for my first child makes it easier to look back at the other two that are still running. For now, I'm the AAA agent for my Athlete, Aerialist, and Author.

Sometimes the unwanted events turn out to be really good experiences. Those are the little clouds with silver linings—not the dramatic thunderstorms that come with a painful tsunami on top, an unthinkable tornado on the side, and a hurricane of sadness, such as the death of a loved one. Or seeing your child sick at the hospital, like Jaume's friend, a twelve-year-old boy who battled with cancer for a year. That, my dear readers, I wish would never happen to anyone. And I wish that with all my being. The negative events I'm talking about are manageable dark clouds, acid lemons.

I've noticed that all the dreams I fought for, broke barriers to achieve, and jumped through hoops to accomplish, have been my most difficult experiences in life. In my case, I didn't want many of the events life threw at me, and yet they led toward the easiest path. These past unwanted eighteen years have been the best.

I planned, and thank God, He laughed, taking care of the rest. He gave me my son, my first lemon—what a great lemonade!

ACKNOWLEDGMENTS

I am so appreciative to my uncle Salvador, a doctor in psychology who left this earth too soon. Thank you for stopping those who judged me and questioned me by telling them, "Are you listening? She says she wants the best for her kids." I will never forget that day.

I am indebted to Marilyn. Without her, Jaume would not have had such a great learning opportunity and such an outstanding role model.

Endless thank you to my editor, my son Jaume, who made this book readable. Without him I would not have been brave enough to write these stories.

Thank you to Argyle Fox Publishing for accepting, editing, and publishing this book. Daniel, the day you emailed me expressing you were interested in my book was the exact day my son turned eighteen. It was a birthday full of happy emotions. My son becoming an adult and my book being born, both on the same day!

Thank you to my husband, Brian. He normally protests all my new adventures, but for this particular one, writing a book, he was encouraging.

Thank you to my parents, who paid for numerous English lessons while growing up so I could be proficient in English. I'm grateful for you!

Thank you, Cayce, for the endless conversations we had weekly at your pool during summertime. I imagined talking to you while writing this book.

And thank you to the people I encountered through the years who spoke powerful things to me through the years. Some of the most memorable include the following:

"Read, read, read to your kids and model reading. Eventually, they will end up reading."

"If the kid wants to pass the tests to go to college, it only takes eighteen months, more or less, to learn the material."

"I was homeschooled and went to college."

"I was unschooled and went to college."

"Disschool yourself."

"Don't do any schooling for a while and see where their passion leads you."

"You can't do worse than the school."